EFFECTIVE ACADEMIC WRITING 2

THE SHORT ESSAY

ALICE SAVAGE
North Harris College
Houston, Texas

PATRICIA MAYER
Teachers College, Columbia University
New York, NY

OXFORD
UNIVERSITY PRESS

OXFORD

UNIVERSITY PRESS

198 Madison Avenue
New York, NY 10016 USA

Great Clarendon Street, Oxford OX2 6DP UK

Oxford University Press is a department of the University of Oxford.
It furthers the University's objective of excellence in research, scholarship,
and education by publishing worldwide in

Oxford New York

Auckland Cape Town Dar es Salaam Hong Kong Karachi
Kuala Lumpur Madrid Melbourne Mexico City Nairobi
New Delhi Shanghai Taipei Toronto

With offices in

Argentina Austria Brazil Chile Czech Republic France Greece
Guatemala Hungary Italy Japan Poland Portugal Singapore
South Korea Switzerland Thailand Turkey Ukraine Vietnam

OXFORD and OXFORD ENGLISH are registered trademarks of
Oxford University Press

Library of Congress Cataloging-in-Publication Data

Savage, Alice,
    Effective academic writing 2 : the short essay / Alice Savage, Patricia Mayer.
        p. cm.
    ISBN-13: 978-0-19-430923-3 (student book)
    1. English language—Rhetoric—Problems, exercises, etc. 2. Essay—
Authorship—Problems, exercises, etc. 3. Report writing—Problems, exercises,
etc. I. Title: Effective academic writing two. II. Mayer, Patricia, III. Title.

PE1471.S28 2006
808'.042—dc22   2005030686

Executive Publisher: Janet Aitchison
Senior Acquisitions Editor: Pietro Alongi
Associate Editor: Scott Allan Wallick
Art Director: Maj-Britt Hagsted
Art Editor: Justine Eun
Production Manager: Shanta Persaud
Production Controller: Zai Jawat Ali

ISBN: 978 0 19 430923 3 (STUDENT BOOK)

Printed in Hong Kong

10 9 8 7 6 5 4 3

ACKNOWLEDGMENTS

Cover art:
Richard Diebenkorn
Ocean Park #122; 1980
oil and charcoal on canvas; 100 in. x 80 5/8 in. (254 cm x204.79 cm)
San Francisco Museum of Modern Art
Charles H. Land Familiar Foundation Fund purchase
© Estate of Richard Diebenkorn

We would like to thank the following for their permission to reproduce photographs:
Alamy: Stock Connection Blue, 28; SHOUT, 54 (new parents); Blend Images:
54 (graduate); Corbis: Christopher Felver, 2 (Joan Didion); Getty Images: Alan
Becker/The Image Bank, 80; Andrew K Davey/Stone, 130 (man with house);
Hulton Archive/Stringer, 2 (F. Scott Fitzgerald); Javier Pierini/Photodisc Red,
130 (man with car); Imagestate: Michel BARET/RAPHO, 106 (lecture); Patrick
Ramsey, 106 (classroom); Library of Congress, Prints and Photographs Division,
FSA-OWI Collection, LC-USF33-030527, 55.

Acknowledgements

Our thanks to the editorial team: Kimberly Steiner, Kenna Bourke, and Scott Allan Wallick for their insight and expertise, and to Pietro Alongi for his endless positivity and for getting us involved in this project. We also want to gratefully acknowledge the work of Susan Kesner Bland. Last but not least, our gratitude to the following reviewers for their contribution to the project: Sharon Allerson, East Los Angeles College; Frank Cronin, Austin Community College; Kieran Hilu, Virginia Tech; Peter Hoffman, LaGuardia Community College; Carla Nyssen, California State University, Long Beach; Adrianne Ochoa; Mary O'Neill, Northern Virginia Community College; Maria Salinas, Del Mar College.

I would like to thank the administration, faculty, and staff of North Harris College for making it such a great place to work. I especially want to applaud the students of the ESL program for being such a joy to teach. Your papers are full of delightful surprises and interesting insights. Thank you for allowing your work to be used to assist others. Finally, I wish to thank my family—Masoud, Cyrus, and Kaveh—for helping me balance work and home. I always look forward to seeing you at the end of the day.
A.S.

First and foremost, I would like to thank Robert Cohen and Kim Sanabria for their constant enthusiasm, encouragement, and camaraderie. Thanks are also due to the CUNY Language Immersion Program students and staff, whose creativity and dedication inspired many of the activities in this book. Lastly, and most importantly, I am and will always be most grateful to Jorge Rosero, Ann Gardner, and Sebastian Rosero-Mayer who will always be my greatest sources of inspiration.
P.M.

Contents

Unit 3: Narrative Essays

Unit 4: Opinion Essays

Unit 5: Comparison and Contrast Essays

Unit 6: Cause and Effect Essays

Appendices

Introduction

Effective Academic Writing is a three-book series intended to usher students into the world of academic writing. The goal of the series is to provide students and their teachers with a practical and efficient approach to learning the skills, strategies, and knowledge that are necessary for succeeding in content coursework. A parallel goal is to provide opportunities for students to explore their opinions, discuss their ideas, and share their experiences through written communication. By guiding budding writers through the experience of composing various types of short papers, we hope to provide students with the tools and the confidence necessary for college success.

The Short Essay

Book 2 of *Effective Academic Writing, The Short Essay,* introduces students at the intermediate level to three- and four-paragraph essays. The first unit provides a thorough review of paragraph structure and mechanics to consolidate knowledge before moving on to more extended writing. Each of the following five units then addresses a particular rhetorical mode and provides user-friendly guidance to mastering the form. The book also offers numerous opportunities for practicing relevant language points.

All language presentations and practice are correlated to *Grammar Sense 2.*

Book 2 contains several features designed to support students in developing the skills that they need for college writing:

- Each unit contains an adapted authentic text to provide ideas and context for the assignment.

- At strategic points in the unit, students read and analyze authentic student essays to see how other students have written on the same or similar topics.

- Each unit contains concise and effective language presentations designed to develop students' understanding of rhetorical modes, and to improve their grammatical accuracy.

- Each unit offers useful writing outlines so that students can learn to plan and to structure their writing.

- Each unit offers collaborative learning activities allowing students to work together and share ideas.

- At relevant points in the unit, editing exercises and editing checklists are provided so that students can refine their writing.

- Timed writing activities come at the close of each unit to prepare students for in-class writing.

- A series of learner-friendly appendices are provided at the back of the book to encourage student independence. A glossary of common grammar terms for student reference is included.

Unit Organization

Each unit introduces a theme and a writing task and then guides the writer through a five-part process of gathering ideas, organizing an outline, drafting, revising, and editing. As students write, they practice specific skills and put language knowledge to work to produce a short paper that follows academic conventions. The rhetorical and language-related goals of the unit are identified on the opener page.

Part 1

Part 1 opens with an image or a quote to spark interest as students begin thinking about the topic. This is followed by a short passage adapted from an authentic text. Students answer questions about the passage that will help them connect the writer's ideas to their own knowledge and experience. They then move on to a free-writing activity, an unstructured writing task in which they can explore the topic without worrying about organization or grammar.

Part 2

In Part 2 students are introduced to a specific rhetorical mode. They begin by brainstorming ideas and vocabulary that they will use to write their essay. They then learn about rhetorical organizational features and read and analyze a student essay. Finally, students produce an outline for the essay they will write later in the unit.

Part 3

In Part 3 students develop the ideas from their outline and produce a first draft. This part opens with a second student essay for students to analyze. As they answer questions about the second student model, students review the organizational features learned in Part 2. They are then introduced to specific, level-appropriate language points that will help students shape and structure their writing. Students now write their first draft and, using a peer-review checklist, check each other's writing for organization and clarity of ideas.

Part 4

In Part 4 students edit their writing and produce a final draft. This part focuses on particular grammar trouble spots relevant to the theme and the rhetorical style presented in the unit. Following the concise language presentation, students complete practice exercises to help them develop their grammar skills and build confidence. The last exercise always focuses on accuracy and involves editing a piece of writing. Students then move on to editing their own writing, and producing a final draft.

Part 5

The final part of the unit is titled "Putting It All Together." This is the summary of the other parts of the unit. Through a series of skill exercises, students review the points covered in Parts 1–4. They are then given the opportunity to write a timed essay using a similar rhetorical focus, but on a different topic. Guidelines for using their time efficiently are suggested. This part also provides students with a comprehensive checklist to review what they have written. The unit closes with suggested tasks for future writing.

Unit 1

Paragraph to Short Essay

Unit Goals

Rhetorical focus:
- paragraph structure
- unity and coherence in a paragraph
- the paragraph and short essay
- short essay organization

Language focus:
- simple and compound sentences
- run-on sentences
- dependent clauses

PART 1

The Paragraph

The reason one writes isn't the fact he wants to say something. He writes because he has something to say.
— F. Scott Fitzgerald

I write entirely to find out what I'm thinking, what I'm looking at, what I see and what it means. What I want and what I fear.
— Joan Didion

A. **Read the quotes about writing. Why did these professional writers write? Do you share their feelings in any way?**

B. **Now discuss the quotes in small groups. Make notes about your feelings on writing. As a group, present your views on writing.**

Rhetorical Focus

Review of Paragraph Structure

A paragraph is a group of sentences about a topic. A typical paragraph begins with a topic sentence, which introduces the topic. The supporting sentences that follow support the idea in the topic sentence with explanations, reasons, and other details. The concluding sentence brings the paragraph to an end.

Formatting a Paragraph

- Leave one-inch margins on the left and right side of the page.

- Indent the first sentence. The rest of the sentences follow each other, so that the paragraph looks like a square with a little space taken out of the corner.

- Double-space your paragraph.

Identifying the elements of a student paragraph

A. Read the paragraph. Then label the formatting elements of the paragraph. Use the words in the box.

a. double spacing	b. margin	c. indent

The Ice-Man

1. _____ → Whenever I remember my experience in the Mexican Air Force, I think of my flight instructor because he taught me how to fly a fighter jet. His nickname was Ice-Man, because he was always calm.

2. _____ → This was a positive characteristic because he had to teach students not to panic in a dangerous situation. For example, one time, I made

3. _____ < a big mistake while we were flying in the clouds. Most instructors would take control and fix the situation, but not Ice-Man. He just gave instructions to fix the problem. I corrected the mistake and got confidence in my abilities. I will always remember his quiet, clear voice and the black aviator glasses that he wore. He was a special person in my life, and I hope that someday I can see him again and thank him for helping me to realize my dream of flying solo and becoming a real pilot.

B. Answer the questions about the paragraph above. Give reasons for your answers.

1. Circle the topic sentence. Does the topic sentence help you understand what the paragraph will be about?

2. How many supporting sentences does the paragraph have? Underline them.

3. Do all the supporting sentences relate to the topic sentence?

4. Circle the concluding sentence. Does the concluding sentence make the paragraph feel finished?

Reading a student paragraph

Read the paragraph. What is the risk that the boy takes?

The Coconut Tree

When I was a boy and first learning about the world, I took a big risk. I was playing in the yard outside of my family's house with my friends. It was a hot day, and we were resting in the shady side of our house. One of my friends dared me to climb the coconut tree in our yard. I looked at the tree. It was mature and very tall, but a little bit curved. I had seen men climbing these trees, and it looked easy, but I had never tried before. I wanted to show my courage, so I said I would. The tree was scratchy, but I found places for my feet and hands and soon I was near the top. But then the tree began to move in the breeze. Suddenly I fell. There was a great pain in my arm. My friends ran to tell my mother who took me to the hospital. I had a broken arm, and one of my ribs was broken. I felt bad for a long time after that. And the worst part was that every day I had to walk past the coconut tree and remember my foolish risk.

Exercise 3 **Analyzing the student paragraph**

A. Answer the questions about the paragraph above.

1. Underline the topic sentence. Is it the first or second sentence? _____
2. Is the first sentence indented? _____
3. How many supporting sentences are there? Which are they? _____
4. Circle the concluding sentence.

B. Respond to the paragraph by answering the following questions.

1. Where was the writer? _____

2. Who was he with? _____

3. What was the consequence of the risk he took? _____

_____

4. Have you ever done something risky? What? _____

_____

The Topic Sentence

An effective paragraph contains a good topic sentence. A successful topic sentence has the following features:

- It introduces the topic, or what the paragraph will be about. It also contains an idea or opinion about the topic. This idea is called a controlling idea about the topic.

  Certain types of **insects** <u>can benefit a garden</u>.

- The topic sentence must not be a simple fact or detail. Instead, it must contain a specific idea. The idea or opinion must not be too general, or the topic sentence will be unclear.

  There are approximately 4,000 chemicals in cigarette smoke. *(fact, not topic sentence)*

  Smoking is bad. *(idea too general for a topic sentence)*

  Smoking advertisements are a harmful influence on children. *(specific idea)*

- The topic sentence usually appears as the first or second sentence of a paragraph. Here it is the second sentence.

  Have you ever noticed that closets are getting bigger and rooms are getting smaller? <u>Changes in popular culture can be seen in changes to the typical family home.</u>

- The topic sentence implies the purpose of the paragraph: to explain, narrate, compare, describe, tell cause or effect, demonstrate or argue, or tell steps in a process.

  My sister's personality is completely different from mine. *(shows comparison)*

  Smoking results in thousands of smoking-related deaths each year. *(tells cause and effect)*

Exercise 4   Identifying topics and controlling ideas

Circle the topic and underline the controlling idea in the topic sentences below.

1. (The painting *Starry Night*) by Vincent Van Gogh <u>is fascinating in many ways.</u>
2. My first driving lesson was a disaster.
3. The process of getting a driver's license has several steps.
4. My ability to speak English has changed my life in several important ways.
5. Some computer games involve the player in physical activity.
6. Cloudy weather affects certain people in negative ways.

Identifying purpose in topic sentences

Identify the purpose of the paragraph that follows logically from each topic sentence below.

1. Almost anyone can get a good grade if they follow these instructions.

    a. express an opinion   b. (tell steps in a process)   c. narrate a story

2. There are three major causes of obesity in children.

    a. compare two subjects   b. explain causes / effects   c. describe a topic

3. I will always remember a fishing trip that I took with my father when I was 12 years old.

    a. compare two subjects   b. explain causes / effects   c. narrate a story

4. I believe that students should not own credit cards.

    a. tell steps in a process   b. explain causes / effects   c. express an opinion

5. Owls are different from hawks in several significant ways.

    a. compare two subjects   b. describe a topic   c. express an opinion

6. My dog, Sparky, is my best friend.

    a. tell steps in a process   b. describe a subject   c. narrate a story

Predicting paragraphs from controlling ideas

Circle the topic and underline the controlling idea of each topic sentence below. Then with a partner, predict what the rest of the paragraph will discuss.

1. (Immigrating to the United States from Vietnam) was difficult for my parents.

    Prediction: _A narrative about the writer's parents' journey from Vietnam to the U.S._

2. Cell phones should not be allowed in classrooms for several reasons.

    Prediction: _____

    _____

3. Cancún Restaurant has the best seafood in town.

    Prediction: _____

    _____

4. Training for the marathon is a complicated process.

    Prediction: _____

    _____

5. Taking the TOEFL is a hardship for many students.

    Prediction: _____

    _____

Identifying effective topic sentences

Read each pair of sentences. Write *TS* next to the sentence that is more effective. Be prepared to explain your choice.

1. _TS_ a. An English-English dictionary is the best choice for English learners.

   _____ b. Many English learners use dictionaries.

2. _____ a. The grains of rice should not stick together.

   _____ b. Persian rice is only considered authentic if it is made in the following way.

3. _____ a. The Internet has changed the way students do research for term papers.

   _____ b. The Internet is changing students' lives.

4. _____ a. A college degree is important.

   _____ b. Having a college degree has many positive effects on a person's life.

Exercise 8 **Writing effective topic sentences**

A. Rewrite each topic sentence so it has both a topic and a controlling idea. Write the revised topic sentence in the left-hand column of the chart. The first one is done for you.

1. **Topic Sentence:** I have an older brother.

Revised topic sentence: My older brother is a great soccer player.	Topic: My older brother
	Controlling idea: is a great soccer player.
	This paragraph will be about: why he is a great soccer player. For example, maybe he has a lot of stamina. He might be good at passing the ball. Or he might be a very effective team player.

2. **Topic Sentence:** Many students eat a lot of fast food.

Revised topic sentence:	Topic:
	Controlling idea:
	This paragraph will be about:

3. **Topic Sentence:** There is a beach near my house.

Revised topic sentence:	Topic:
	Controlling idea:
	This paragraph will be about:

4. **Topic Sentence:** Many teenagers go shopping.

Revised topic sentence:	Topic:
	Controlling idea:
	This paragraph will be about:

5. **Topic Sentence:** Hurricanes hit Florida every year.

Revised topic sentence:	Topic:
	Controlling idea:
	This paragraph will be about:

B. Now exchange books with a partner. Read each revised topic sentence, and write its topic and controlling idea in the right-hand column of the chart. Then write what you think the paragraph will be about. When you have finished, discuss with your partner.

In Part 2, you will …

• learn about paragraph unity and coherence.

PART 2

Unity and Coherence

Rhetorical Focus

Unity Within a Paragraph

Effective writing must have unity. A paragraph has unity when all the sentences support one single idea:

- The paragraph must have one controlling idea in the topic sentence. Otherwise, the paragraph loses focus.

- The supporting sentences must support, demonstrate, prove, or develop the main idea in the topic sentence. If they do not, they will be irrelevant or off-topic and destroy the unity of the paragraph.

- The concluding sentence should restate the idea in the topic sentence to reinforce the main idea for the reader.

Exercise 1 | **Reading a student paragraph**

Read the paragraph. What is the talent of each of the three family members described in the paragraph?

Stories of Nepal

My mother grew up in a creative and interesting family in Nepal. Her father was an astronomer who worked for the King of Nepal. Very often he would take her to work with him so she could look through a telescope and see the planets and stars. Then she would play in the planetarium until her older brother came to pick her up. On the walk home, her brother would tell her stories. Sometimes he would point to someone on the street or standing in a doorway and tell her that the stranger was a magician or a time-traveler and begin a new story about the person. My grandmother was also interesting. She liked to paint portraits of children. She painted many beautiful portraits of my mother and her cat, Sani, although my mother said it was difficult to sit still. After my mother left Nepal, she studied computer programming in Wisconsin. I love to remember my mother's stories, and now I enjoy telling my own daughter about her grandmother's life in Nepal.

Analyzing the student paragraph for unity

Examine the organization of the paragraph by answering the questions below. Then compare your answers with a partner.

1. Underline the topic sentence. Is it the first or second sentence? _____

2. Write the controlling idea from the topic sentence in your own words.

   _____

   _____

3. One sentence in the paragraph is irrelevant. Draw a line through it.

4. Why is the sentence irrelevant? Write your explanation below:

   _____

   _____

Recognizing unity in supporting sentences

Read the following topic sentences. Put a check (✓) next to each sentence below that supports the topic sentence.

1. There are several reasons why online courses are increasing in popularity.

   __✓__ a. Online courses are flexible in terms of time.

   _____ b. Online courses have been available since the 1990s.

   __✓__ c. Online courses are more convenient for students who live far away from the campus.

2. Childhood diabetes has many possible causes.

   _____ a. Obesity is a major cause of diabetes.

   _____ b. Children who eat too much sugar can get diabetes.

   _____ c. Children with diabetes need constant medical care.

3. The best way to reduce traffic in our city is to build a metro subway system.

   _____ a. Pollution is very bad in our city.

   _____ b. Widening the freeways has not solved the problem of traffic congestion.

   _____ c. A metro subway system would encourage people to take public transportation to work.

4. I am afraid of dogs because I had a scary experience with one when I was ten.

    ____ a. My children are not allowed to have a pet dog.

    ____ b. My neighbor owned a collie dog that ran around the neighborhood without a leash.

    ____ c. The dog bit me.

5. Scenic Beach is my favorite picnic spot because of its beauty.

    ____ a. It is a quiet narrow beach covered with oyster shells.

    ____ b. One time I had an interesting experience there.

    ____ c. The Olympic Mountains rise straight up out of the water on the other side of the channel.

6. Train stations are interesting places to visit.

    ____ a. The architecture of each train station is often connected to the history of a city.

    ____ b. The passengers are frequently more interesting to watch than other types of travelers.

    ____ c. Trains are a good alternative for people who are afraid of flying.

7. The world of dinosaurs is very familiar to the general population.

    ____ a. Scientists believe that the birds of today are descended from dinosaurs.

    ____ b. Every year, new movies and TV shows about dinosaurs are produced.

    ____ c. Children study dinosaurs and play with dinosaur toys from an early age.

Exercise 4   Editing for unity

Read the paragraph. Draw a line through the sentences that are irrelevant. The first one is done for you. Find three more.

I love to watch the pelicans in Galveston. I usually go in the winter. ~~The weather is not warm enough for swimming, so I usually do not see many people on the beach.~~ Pelicans are not elegant, but they are interesting to watch. They remind me of prehistoric birds from my school textbook on dinosaurs. I studied dinosaurs a lot when I was young, and I am very fond of them. The pelicans have large grayish-brown wings that bend sharply when they are flying, and their beaks are long, so their faces look peculiar and old. My brother also really likes pelicans. They are also graceful in their own way. A flock of pelicans will fly along the coastline just outside the waves, and when they see a good fishing spot, they stop, then turn and dive straight down into the water. Sometimes there is an oil rig or a cargo ship in the water, too. Sometimes several pelicans will fish in the same spot for a while before moving down the beach and away from sight.

Exercise 5   **Developing unity**

Write two or three supporting sentences for each of the following topic sentences. Then exchange books with a partner and check your partner's sentences for unity.

1. Joining a sports team can provide many benefits. _____

    _____

    _____

    _____

2. My first day in my new school was full of surprises. _____

    _____

    _____

    _____

3. A road trip is the best way to see the United States. _____

    _____

    _____

    _____

4. Many people do not realize that packing a suitcase requires skill and planning.

    _____

    _____

    _____

Coherence in a Paragraph

Coherence in a paragraph means that the ideas have a logical flow: the relationship between the sentences is clear and one idea connects to the next. One way to achieve coherence in a paragraph is to use a pattern of organization, such as time order, spatial order, or order of importance.

Exercise 6 **Reading a student paragraph**

Read the paragraph. How many rules does the writer give?

Important Rules for Acting On Stage

For people who would like to act in the theater, there are several important rules to remember. One rule, often forgotten, is to make sure you face your audience when you are on stage. If you turn away from the audience, they cannot see your facial expressions. Next, make sure that you speak loudly enough. If your audience has difficulty hearing you, they will quickly lose interest. Another important point is to memorize your lines. Rehearse them often—on the train, in the mirror, while you are walking to class—so that you remember them. Finally, perhaps the most important rule of all is to remain calm on stage if you forget your lines. Don't panic and stop speaking because the audience will notice. Instead, make up something to say until you remember your next line. As long as you continue speaking and appear relaxed, the audience will probably not realize that you have made a mistake. In conclusion, following these rules will help ensure a successful stage performance.

Exercise 7 **Analyzing the student paragraph for coherence**

Examine the organization of the paragraph by answering the questions below. Then compare your answers with a partner.

1. Underline the topic sentence.

2. What should an actor do if he forgets his lines? _____

_____

3. The writer uses order of importance as a pattern of coherence. Do the ideas move from more important to less important or less important to more important? _____

_____

Exercise 8 **Reordering for coherence**

Read the sentences from a narrative paragraph. Some of the sentences are out of order. Number the sentences from 1–10 to show logical time order. Then compare your answers with a partner.

_____ a. My family hugged me and cried because I had been gone so long.

__1__ b. I will never forget one day when I had to travel alone on the subway.

_____ c. I was pregnant, and I had to go to an appointment at the hospital.

_____ d. When my appointment ended, I got on the subway to go home.

_____ e. That was why my surroundings looked unfamiliar.

_____ f. My appointment was at 1:00 p.m.

_____ g. Suddenly I looked up and did not know where I was.

_____ h. I was exhausted and fell asleep on my way home.

_____ i. Then I realized that I had fallen asleep.

_____ j. It took me five more hours to get back to my home.

In Part 3, you will …

• learn about short essay structure and organization.
• practice writing a thesis statement.

From Paragraph to Short Essay

Rhetorical Focus

The Paragraph and the Short Essay

A short essay is longer than a paragraph, but like a paragraph it has three basic parts: an introduction, a body, and a conclusion.

- Introduction: the introductory paragraph is the first paragraph of a short essay. It contains a topic sentence and thesis statement.

- Body paragraph: A short essay has at least one or two body paragraphs. These develop the idea presented in the introduction.

- Conclusion: The concluding paragraph is the final paragraph and summaries the idea(s) presented in the short essay.

Compare the similar ways that a paragraph and a short essay function.

Paragraph		Short Essay
The topic sentence states the topic.	⟶	The introductory paragraph states the topic.
The topic sentence states the the controlling idea.	⟶	The thesis statement states the controlling idea.
The supporting sentences of the paragraph support the idea in the topic sentence.	⟶	The body paragraphs support the idea in the thesis statement. Each body paragraph has a topic sentence.
The concluding sentence summarizes the idea in the topic sentence.	⟶	The essay conclusion summarizes the idea in the thesis statement.

Read the paragraph and then the short essay. Which is more interesting?

Paragraph	Short Essay
My uncle Patricio is one of the most interesting people in my family. He is old and has a wrinkled brown face. On his arm, there is a tattoo. Patricio has an intriguing history. He and my mother were born in a small village in the mountains. When he was seventeen, he left home to explore the world. Now he fixes air conditioners in Los Angeles, and during the winter months, he sometimes comes to visit us and play the accordion. I love spending time with my uncle Patricio because he has an interesting look and a mysterious past. Someday, I hope that he will tell me more about his life.	My family is full of happy, crazy, and talented people. My aunt Margarita has a yard full of orphaned pets. My brother José is an expert tailor, and my mother loves to experiment in the kitchen. However, I think the most interesting is my mysterious uncle Patricio. **introduction** Patricio is an elderly man now, with white hair sticking up all over his head. Beneath his messy hair, he has a wrinkled brown face and powerful dark eyes that show many emotions. Patricio is tall and skinny, and he wears baggy pants and a plaid shirt. He has a tattoo of a heart on his arm. The heart has the word Rosa written across it in red and black letters, but he has never told me who she is. **body paragraph 1** Patricio has an intriguing history. He and my mother were born in a small village in the mountains. When he was seventeen, he left home to explore the world. On one trip, he went to Siberia to look for gold. On another trip, he went to Alaska to work on a fishing boat. Now he fixes air conditioners in Los Angeles, and during the winter months, he sometimes comes to visit us and play the accordion. **body paragraph 2** I love spending time with my uncle Patricio. He has an interesting look and a sad and mysterious past. He is also a talented musician. Someday, I hope that he will tell me about Rosa and how he got the tattoo with her name. **conclusion**

| Exercise 2 | **Analyzing the paragraph and short essay** |

Answer the questions about the paragraph and short essay on page 16.

1. What information is included in the short essay introduction that is not in the topic sentence of the paragraph ?_____

   _____

2. Write the topic and controlling idea of body paragraph 1 in your own words.

   _____

3. What new details have been added to body paragraph 1 in the essay?

   _____

4. Write the topic and controlling idea of body paragraph 2 in your own words.

   _____

5. What additional details have been added to body paragraph 2 in the essay?

   _____

6. What information is included in the essay conclusion that is not in the concluding sentence of the paragraph? _____

   _____

Rhetorical Focus

Short Essay Organization

An effective essay must have the following elements.

Introduction
- A hook is an opening sentence that attracts the reader's attention.
- The sentences after the hook give background information necessary to understand the topic.
- The last sentence in the introduction, the thesis statement, is very important because it gives the topic and the controlling idea of the entire essay.

Body Paragraph
- An essay has at least one body paragraph in which the writer develops the thesis statement from the introduction. The body paragraph begins with a topic sentence, followed by supporting details.

Conclusion
- An essay ends with a conclusion that summarizes or restates the main idea in the thesis statement.

Understanding thesis statements

A. **Read the short essay. The thesis statement is missing. Choose the best thesis statement from the list following the essay. Discuss your choice with a partner.**

Imagine having a job that fits your class schedule. You do not have conflicts with studying because you only work at night and on the weekends. In addition, you can work in a beautiful room with paintings on the walls, candlelight, and beautiful music playing in the background. _____

_____

First, restaurant work is a great job for a student because the hours are different. Most restaurants are busiest during the weekends in the evening. Since students have to go to class during the week and during the day, a restaurant job gives them time for class.

The second reason why restaurant work suits students is that the student can eat at the restaurant. Students are short on time. They don't want to go shopping, cook, or clean up, so they need to get meals in a hurry. It is perfect if they can eat at work.

Students can make money, eat, and still have time for class if they work in a restaurant. For this reason, many eating places are staffed by students. It's a great job for those who need to work while they are in college.

---

a. A restaurant job is a convenient choice for a college student for several reasons.

b. Many restaurants hire college students.

c. A college student can make a lot of money working in an expensive restaurant.

B. Now read this short essay. The thesis statement is missing. Write a thesis statement on the lines provided. Make sure your thesis states a topic and a controlling idea. Compare your answer with a partner.

I have many wonderful memories of my childhood in El Salvador, but I have one memory that still makes me shiver when I think about it. I lived with my grandmother in a house in the country, and I had many cousins to play with. The neighbors all knew me, and we children always felt safe. _____

_____

My scary experience happened when I was about ten. I was playing hide and seek with some children from the neighborhood when my cousin and I discovered a dark abandoned warehouse. We were happy because we thought that no one would find us there. We went inside. There were boxes, and everything was covered with dust. Suddenly my cousin ran away. I thought she was hiding, so I laughed and called her name, but she did not answer. I started to hide too, but at that moment, I smelled a terrible odor. I looked in the corner, and a big shape was moving. It was dark, and I couldn't see very well, but I knew it was big. I ran outside as fast as I could. My cousin was outside, and we ran back to our house as fast as we could.

I still do not know what was in the warehouse. My grandmother said she thought some thieves had been hiding there. She said it was a lucky thing that they didn't see me. Her words made me more afraid. I thought, "what if they had caught me?" After that, I decided to stay away from that dark warehouse. I learned to be very careful and never go into empty buildings again, no matter what!

In Part 4 you will ...
- review simple and compound sentences.
- learn about main and dependent clauses.
- learn how to correct run-on sentences.

Language Focus

The Sentence

A sentence contains at least one subject (a noun or a phrase) and a verb, and expresses a complete idea. The verb expresses the action of the sentence, and the subject tells who or what completed the action. A simple sentence may contain more than one noun or verb.

Subject	Verb
My **dog**	**runs**.
My **dog**	**runs** and **chases** squirrels. *(two verbs)*
My **dog** and **cat**	**run** after squirrels. *(two nouns in subject)*

A complete sentence must contain at least one main clause. A main clause contains a subject and a verb, and expresses a complete idea.

The Simple Sentence

A simple sentence, shown below, contains one main clause.

Subject	Verb
My **dog**	**runs** after squirrels.

The Compound Sentence

A compound sentence has two main clauses, separated by a comma and a conjunction, or by a semicolon.

Main Clause	Conjunction	Main Clause
My dog runs after squirrels,	**and**	the squirrels run away.
My dog terrifies the squirrels,	**so**	they stay high in the trees.
My dog chases them everyday,	**but**	he has never caught one.
The squirrels climb trees,	**or**	they sometimes run through fences.

Main Clause	Main Clause
My dog is very clever;	he can do many tricks.

Identifying clauses

Read the sentences. Then circle the number of clauses contained in each sentences.

1. The fish were hungry.   1   2

2. The fish were hungry, and they ate the food quickly.   1   2

3. I love to go to the park, so I try to go every weekend.   1   2

4. The bus takes a long time, but it is less expensive than a car. 1   2

5. Computers are very important today; they can do many things. 1   2

6. I want to marry a man with a good education and an
   honest character.   1   2

Language Focus

Run-on Sentences

A run-on sentence is not a correct sentence. In a run-on sentence, important punctuation is missing between the clauses. The sentence "runs on" too long and confuses the reader.

• You can correct run-on sentences with a period, a comma and conjunction, or a semicolon.

My dog runs fast he likes to chase animals in the park. (INCORRECT)
My dog runs fast. He likes to chase animals in the park.
My dog runs fast, **and** he likes to chase animals in the park.

My dog is difficult to take care of still I love him very much. (INCORRECT)
My dog is difficult to take care of; **still**, I love him very much.
My dog means a lot to me; he is my best friend.

Correcting run-on sentences with conjunctions

The following sentences are run-on sentences. Rewrite them as complete sentences by adding the conjunctions *and, or, so,* or *but.*

1. I am busy with work I am studying. _I am busy with work, or I am studying._

2. Almost everyone in her neighborhood speaks her language she does not
   have to use English. _____

   _____

3. Credit cards are convenient they are also dangerous. _____

   _____

4. I did not have experience I tried to get a job. _____

   _____

5. Every time I travel, either I take a suitcase I take a backpack. _____

   _____

6. My lucky number is seven my favorite color is red. _____

   _____

Language Focus

> ### Dependent Clauses
>
> A dependent clause is a clause that is not a complete sentence by
> itself. It has a subject and a verb, but it does not have a complete idea.
> A dependent clause often starts with a subordinating conjunction like
> *because, before, since, when, after,* or *while.* A dependent clause must
> always be attached to a main (or independent) clause to make one
> complete sentence. The dependent clause can come before or after the
> main clause without changing the meaning, but the punctuation
> is different.
>
> | dependent clause |
>
> | main clause |
>
> **When I talk to my friend,** she likes to tell me about her adventures.
>
> | main clause |
>
> | dependent clause |
>
> My friend likes to tell me about her adventures **when I talk to her.**

Exercise 3   Identifying dependent and main clauses

**Underline and label the clauses. Write *M* above the main clause in each
sentence. Write *D* above the dependent clause.**

       D   M

1. <u>When I was growing up,</u> <u>everything was less expensive.</u>

2. I guess things have changed since I was younger.

3. I was sad when we left my country.

4. When I am older, I want to have a big house with a patio and a swimming pool.

5. After you understand the meaning of a word, you can practice writing sentences.

6. It is only dangerous when the roads are wet.

7. Because the tide went out, the jellyfish were stranded on the beach.

8. My country was invaded many times before we formed our current government.

Correcting run-on sentences with punctuation

Read the sentences. If the sentence is correct, write *C*. If the sentence is incorrect, write *I* and add correct punctuation, using a comma, semicolon, or period. Check for proper capitalization.

_I_ 1. I went to the store with my friend Rachel. ~~we~~ *We* bought milk.

____ 2. We brought the groceries through the back door after we got back.

____ 3. I noticed that there was a little dirt on the floor the DVD player was missing nothing else was gone.

____ 4. We called the police after we realized there had been a robbery.

____ 5. The police arrived immediately and inspected the whole apartment.

____ 6. They took statements later that afternoon they found the robbers and Rachel's DVD player.

Exercise 5 **Editing a paragraph**

Read the paragraph and edit as necessary. Correct the run-on sentences. There are six mistakes.

I am the middle child in my family I wish I were not sometimes. My brother and sisters have an easier life than I do. My older brother is very responsible he is like a third parent my sisters and I have to do what he tells us if our parents are not home. He also has more freedom than we do. He can go out on the weekends and stay out late we have to be at home by 10:00 p.m. While my brother has more freedom than I do, my sisters have an easier life. They are twins they get a lot of attention from our parents. My parents don't often spend time with me they spend most of their time with my sisters. Because I am not the oldest, I do not have the same power as my brother, but I do not get the extra attention either. As a result, I think the middle child is not lucky at all.

In Part 5 you will:

- review topics and controlling ideas.
- review unity.
- practice identifying thesis statements.
- practice correcting run-on sentences.

PART 5

Putting It All together

Exercise 1   Identifying topics and controlling ideas

Circle the topic and underline the controlling idea in the topic sentences below.

1. Pizza is easy to make if you follow these steps.
2. If you compare a Mini-Cooper with a Volkswagen Bug, you will find several important differences.
3. There are several ways to reduce stress.
4. Not getting enough sleep can have negative effects on a student.
5. One of my backpacking trips was almost my last.
6. A good journalist has to have special talents and skills.

Exercise 2   Editing a paragraph

Read the paragraph. Draw a line through the sentences that are irrelevant. There are four irrelevant sentences.

> When I want to eat steak, I go to my favorite restaurant, Saltgrass Steakhouse, because I always have a good experience. I love walking through the big heavy wooden doors because the spicy smell of grilled meat makes my mouth water. The hostess knows my family, and she always gives us a good seat where we can watch the other customers and enjoy the cowboy decorations on the walls. The service is friendly and efficient. On the other hand, the cook is often grumpy. He yells at the waiters sometimes. The waiters always bring crayons and paper for my daughters. I always order the rib-eye steak because the grilled meat is tender and seasoned with delicious spices. After dinner, we talk and enjoy the atmosphere. It is not good to eat there every day because the beef has a lot of fat. All red meat has a lot of fat, and it can cause problems such as high cholesterol. I like to eat at Saltgrass Steakhouse once a month, but I would eat there more often if I had the money. It has the best steak in the city.

Identifying thesis statements

Read the short essay. The thesis statement is missing. Choose the best thesis statement from the list following the short essay.

> A good party game that is simple and fun for everyone is zombie tag. Children love it and so do adults because there is no fancy equipment and anyone who can jump can participate. _____
>
> _____
>
> Zombie tag follows the same basic procedure as regular tag with a few additional rules. First, decide on the boundaries. It is a good idea to play outside in a backyard or in a park. Then choose one person to be *It*. *It* must then "tag" another player, and then the tagged player becomes *It*. Finally, in zombie tag all players must keep their arms at their sides and their ankles together. This means that they must jump instead of run, and they must tag with their shoulders or hips rather than their hands. If a player does not keep his ankles together or his arms at his sides, he is cheating and must sit out for five minutes.
>
> In conclusion, zombie tag is a good party game for all ages because it requires no equipment and is easy to play. People usually have a good time because they have to keep their bodies straight and hold their arms at their sides and this makes them look funny when they jump, so they laugh a lot.

a. I often play zombie tag with my friends at birthday parties.

b. Zombie tag is easy to play if you follow the steps below.

c. Zombie tag is different from regular tag in two important ways.

Correcting run-on sentences with punctuation

Read the sentences. If the sentence is correct, write *C*. If the sentence is incorrect, write *I* and add correct punctuation, using a comma, semicolon, or period. Check for proper capitalization.

_____ 1. My father decided to go to dental school he was at the top of his class.

_____ 2. My writing has improved a great deal but I still need to work on my grammar.

_____ 3. When I am an industrial engineer I want to design kitchen appliances.

_____ 4. Secretaries play a very important role in an office; without them many businesses could not function.

_____ 5. I have never been afraid of snakes I think they are beautiful.

_____ 6. We lived in Malaysia after we got married.

Editing a paragraph

Read the paragraph and edit as necessary. There are six mistakes.

The memory of summer vacations at my grandmother's home in Ayutta, Thailand, always makes me happy. I loved this house very much because it was a beautiful and spacious place all the members of my family could gather together and enjoy nature. The house was located on a quiet stretch of river under a clear blue sky. It was a traditional, waterfront, Thai-style home it was built from teak wood. The tall, green trees around the house provided shade along the riverbank. Inside the house, there were many rooms my uncle's and my aunt's families could all come together at the same time. When we woke up, we could hear the sound of singing birds We children always rushed outside to breathe fresh air, and dig our toes into the sand. In the afternoon, we played in the shade of the trees, swam in the river, and dug in the gardens. The adults watched us from the patio they could see us and we could see them. This home was the center place of my family I like to think about it when I feel lonely.

Unit 2

Descriptive Essays

Unit Goals

Rhetorical focus:
- descriptive organization

Language focus:
- prepositional phrases in descriptive writing
- adding details to sentences
- similes
- using adjectives in descriptive writing

Descriptive writing uses words to build images for the reader. These images may come from sights, sounds, smells, tastes, or even feelings. Good descriptive writing makes the reader feel as if he or she is present in the scene.

Exercise 1 **Thinking about the topic**

A. Discuss the picture with a partner.

- What do you think the occasion might be?
- Why is this food special?
- Who are the people in the picture?
- How do they feel?

B. Make notes about food that you and your family eat during family celebrations and special occasions. Then discuss in small groups.

Exercise 2 **Reading about the topic**

Sometimes a single event can have a lasting effect on a person's life. A famous New York chef, Anthony Bourdain, describes a childhood experience with an oyster (a kind of shellfish) during a family vacation in France.

Food is Good

At six in the morning, we climbed into Monsieur Saint-Jour's small wooden boat with our picnic baskets. He was an old man dressed in ancient denim work pants. He had a leathery, tanned and windblown face, **hollow** cheeks, and tiny broken blood vessels on his nose and cheeks. We took the boat out to his underwater oyster park, a fenced-off section of bay bottom, and we sat … and sat … and sat, in the roaring August sun, waiting for the **tide** to go out. The idea was to float the boat over the fence walls, then sit there until the boat slowly sank with the water level until it rested on the bay floor.

There was, I remember, still about two feet of water left to go before the boat settled on dry ground and we could walk around the park. We'd already eaten all the food from our picnic baskets, but I was still hungry, and said so.

Monsieur Saint-Jour asked if any of us would like to try an oyster.

My parents **hesitated**. I doubt they'd realized they might actually have to eat one of the **raw** slimy things we were floating over. My little brother pulled away in horror.

But I, in the proudest moment of my young life, stood up smartly in **defiance**, and volunteered to be the first. And in that sweet moment in my personal history, that one moment still more alive for me than so many of the others, I won glory. Monsieur Saint-Jour reached down into the water and came up holding a single oyster, huge and irregularly shaped, in his rough fist. With an oyster knife, he popped the thing open and handed it to me. Everyone was watching now, my little brother pulling away from this shiny, wet object, still dripping and nearly alive.

I took it in my hand, tipped the shell back into my mouth as instructed by Monsieur Saint-Jour, and with one bite and a slurp, I **wolfed** it down. It tasted of seawater … and flesh … and somehow … of the future.

Bourdain, A. *Kitchen Confidential* (Adapted). New York: Harper Collins, 2000: 15–16.

hollow: empty
tide: the periodic rise and fall of the ocean
hesitate: to pause in doubt

raw: uncooked
defiance: resistance to authority
wolfed: ate very quickly

Understanding the text

Write *T* for true or *F* for false for each statement.

_____ 1. Bourdain rode with his family in a large boat.

_____ 2. When Bourdain and his family arrived at the oyster park, they waited a short time for the water level to go down.

_____ 3. Everyone in the family wanted to try the oysters.

_____ 4. Bourdain was proud of himself for eating the oyster.

Responding to the text

Write your answers for each question in full sentences. Then discuss your answers with a partner.

1. How had Monsieur Saint-Jour's work affected his appearance? _____

   _____

   _____

   _____

2. How do you think Bourdain felt when he first saw the boat? Do you think his feelings changed during the trip? How so? _____

   _____

   _____

   _____

3. How do you think Bourdain described the oyster trip when he returned home? _____

   _____

   _____

   _____

4. What did he mean when he said "it tasted of … the future?" _____

   _____

   _____

   _____

Write for ten to fifteen minutes on the topic below. Express yourself as well as you can. Don't worry about mistakes.

The writer of the passage was the only person in his family who was not afraid to try the oyster. On a separate piece of paper, write about the first time you tried a new food.

- Where were you?
- What food did you try?
- What did it taste, smell, or feel like?
- What was your reaction to it?

In Part 2 you will …

- learn about descriptive organization.
- brainstorm ideas and specific vocabulary to use in your writing.
- create an outline for your essay.

Brainstorming and Outlining

✍ **WRITING TASK**

In this unit, you will write a three-paragraph descriptive essay about a food you feel strongly about—one you really like or dislike.

Exercise 1   **Brainstorming ideas**

Think of a food you really like or dislike. On a separate piece of paper write down your ideas about this food in a word web, like the one below. Think about the food's taste, smell, appearance, preparation, any sounds you associate with it, or the context in which you eat it.

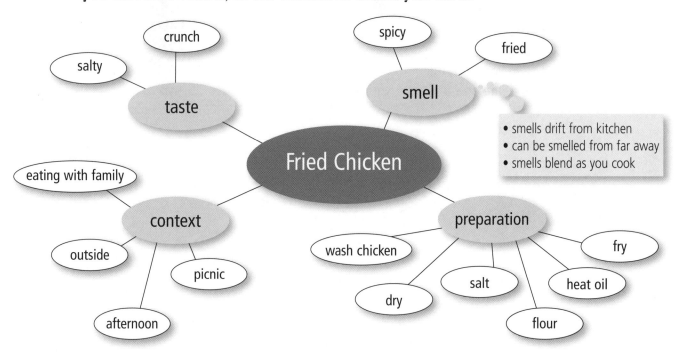

Exercise 2   **Brainstorming vocabulary**

A. **Think about the food you want to write about. Add two more words to each set to describe the food. Then circle the words you would like to use in each set.**

1. **Taste:** salty, sour, bitter, sweet, juicy,_____ ,_____

2. **Touch:** soft, hard, chewy, tough, crunchy,_____ ,_____

3. **Smell:** sweet, comforting, sharp, strong, faint, _____ , _____

4. **Sight:** small, big, tempting, smooth,_____ ,_____

B. **On a separate piece of paper, practice writing these words in sentences. Use your dictionary for help.**

Descriptive Organization

In a descriptive essay, a writer uses details to tell how a subject looks, sounds, smells, tastes, or feels. The essay should make the reader feel like responding to what he or she is reading.

Introduction
- The hook introduces the object or event of description.
- The middle sentences provide the background.
- The thesis statement tells why the object or event of description is important to the writer.

Body Paragraphs
- Most of the description is in the body paragraphs.
- Adjectives and adverbs make the experience more vivid.
- The scene is often described with prepositions and prepositional phrases that specify location or position in space.
- Comparisons, such as similes, can make the writing more descriptive, familiar, and expressive.

Conclusion
- The conclusion gives the writer's final opinion about the description.

Exercise 3   **Reading a student essay**

Read the essay. According to the writer, where can you get the best pizza?

The Best Pizza in Town and Maybe the World

I have suffered a great deal because of a terrible addiction to pizza. Basically, I enjoy pizza too much. In fact, I enjoy it so much, I won't share it, not even with my mother. People in my hometown of Cabimas, Venezuela, laugh at me and call me the Pizza King of Cabimas, but it is a name that I am proud of. I have eaten pizza in many places, and none is as good as the pizza of Cabimas.

The best place to eat pizza in Cabimas is at Papa's. Customers have to wait in line to get a table but the wait is worth it. Once they are seated, pizza-lovers can choose from many varieties of pizza, such as pizza with shrimp and smoked oysters or pizza with pine nuts and garlic, but my favorite is the sausage and pepperoni. First of all, it is big. When the waiter puts it down in front of me, I feel happy because I will get enough to eat. It smells of garlic, oil, and spices. And it looks delicious too. The sauce oozes out from under a layer of rich melted cheese. The best part is the first bite. I sink my teeth into a slightly crunchy crust, thick tomato sauce and gooey cheese, and I am in heaven. I can eat two of these pizzas in one night, even though I know I will have a stomachache afterwards.

Now that I am in the United States, I am trying different kinds of pizzas here. I have never seen so many different pizza restaurants! I want to try them one by one. So far, some of them are delicious, but I am convinced that the best pizza in the world is still at Papa's restaurant a couple of blocks from the house where I grew up.

Exercise 4 **Examining the student essay**

A. Respond to the essay by answering the questions below.

1. What is the main idea of the introduction?
   a. how the author has suffered
   b. pizza
   c. the author's addiction to pizza
   d. the author's hometown

2. Which paragraph has the most descriptive details? _____

3. The conclusion ends with a(n) _____.
   a. description
   b. restatement of the main idea in the introduction
   c. story
   d. invitation

B. Examine the organization of the essay by answering the questions below. Then compare your answers with a partner.

1. What is the author's thesis statement about pizza? _____
   _____

2. What words or phrases does the author use to describe the pizzas? _____
   _____

3. What words or phrases does the author use to show how he feels when he eats pizza? _____
   _____

4. What is the author's final comment about pizza in the conclusion? _____
   _____

Exercise 5   **Completing an outline**

Look back at the essay on pages 33–34. Then, fill in the missing information in the outline below.

Introduction

Topic: _Pizza in Cabimas_ _____

Hook: _I'm addicted to pizza._ _____

Background information: _don't share pizza with anyone, called the Pizza_ ____
King, tried pizza in many places _____

Thesis statement: 1. _____

Body Paragraph

Details: _places to eat pizza, Papa's, types of pizza_ 2. _____
_____

Words or phrases: _gooey, cheesy, rich melted cheese, stomachache, big,_ ____
spices, crunchy crust _____

Conclusion

Final opinion: 3. _____
_____
_____

Writing an outline

Review your brainstorming ideas and your freewriting exercise. Then use the chart below to write an outline for your essay. Use the outline on page 35 as an example.

Introduction

What is your topic? _____

_____

Think of a hook that will engage the reader. _____

_____

_____

Write some notes on relevant background information your reader will need.

_____

_____

_____

What is your thesis statement? _____

_____

_____

Body Paragraph

What details will you include in your description? What words or phrases do you think you will use? _____

_____

_____

_____

_____

Conclusion

What is the final opinion you want to give about your description? _____

_____

_____

_____

In Part 3 you will ...

- learn about prepositional phrases.
- learn to use descriptive details in your writing.
- learn about similes in descriptive writing.
- write a first draft of your descriptive essay.

PART 3

Developing Your Ideas

Reading a student essay

Read the essay. What is the main event the writer describes?

Food from the Sea

My father told me that we should always respect nature and learn where our food comes from. He said that food tasted better when you got it yourself and ate it in a natural place. To show me this was true, he took me to the ocean, where we caught our own delicious crabs and ate them.

I will always remember the taste of the crabs we caught that day. The beach was quiet and still at six o'clock. The tide had just come in, so there were many crabs walking slowly on the white sand. We sat a few feet away from my father's special crab traps. The traps were made of bamboo, and they looked like round cages, but one side had a small entrance for the crab to go in. There were some small, fragrant fish in the trap. The fishy smell made the crabs hungry, so they crawled into the traps. We watched the crabs walk into the traps, and I smelled the strong smell of the dark, oily fish. Overhead, we heard the sounds of seagulls and pelicans in the sky. I think the seagulls wanted to eat the fish, too. Once the traps were full, we took off our shoes and threw them over our shoulders so we could walk on the wet sand and feel the water pushing and pulling at the beach. Later, we built a fire and ate boiled crabs on the beach. We cracked their shells. The meat was white and pinkish and tender. It tasted sweet and a little salty. We did not want to stop eating them. We sat on the sand surrounded by crab shells and watched the sun go down into the ocean.

From that day on, I knew my father was right. Food tastes best when it is something that you have caught or grown yourself. I have eaten crab many times since then, but it has never tasted as good as it did that day.

Examining the student essay

Respond to the essay by answering the questions below in full sentences.

1. What does the place described in the essay look like? _____

   _____

   _____

2. How does the writer feel about his experience? _____

   _____

   _____

3. What sounds, sights, smells, or tastes are described? _____

   _____

   _____

4. What is the final opinion that the writer gives in the conclusion? _____

   _____

   _____

Language Focus

Prepositional Phrases in Descriptive Writing

A prepositional phrase is made up of a preposition + a noun phrase or pronoun.

prepositional phrase		prepositional phrase

The boat slowly sank **with the water level** until it rested **on the bay floor.**

Prepositional phrases are important in descriptive writing. They show the position, location, or direction of objects in space and time. We can also use prepositional phrases to show manner or attitude.

* Prepositional phrases that show position and location:

  The boat slowly sank **with the water level** until it rested **on the bay floor.**

* Prepositional phrases that show direction:

  We took the boat out **to his underwater oyster park.**

  The idea was to float the boat **over the fence walls.**

* Prepositional phrases that show time:

  at six in the morning   **in that sweet moment**   **on Sunday**

* Prepositional phrases that show manner or attitude:

  I stood up **in defiance.**   He pulled back **in horror.**

Identifying prepositional phrases

A. Look at the following sentences. Circle the prepositional phrases.

1. The idea was to float the boat over the fence walls.

2. The boat settled on dry ground.

3. We could walk around the park.

4. He held an oyster in his rough fist.

5. I tipped the shell back into my mouth.

6. It tasted of the future.

B. Look back at the student essay on page 37. Underline the prepositional phrases. Compare your answers with a partner.

Language Focus

Adding Details to Sentences

Details tell what something looks like, or how it sounds, feels, tastes, or smells. We can use nouns, adjectives, adverbs, and verbs to add details. The more specific the details are the more effective and interesting the writing will be. Clear, specific details allow the reader to create a picture in his or her mind of what is being described. Compare the general sentences below with ones that have specific details.

General Sentences	Sentences with Specific Details
The crabs were <u>good</u>.	The crabs were **tender and sweet with a salty taste.**
He bought some <u>fruit</u>.	He bought some **sweet, juicy strawberries.**
She <u>walked</u> to the door.	She **tiptoed** to the door.
She walked to the door.	She walked **quickly and silently** to the door.

Adding specific details

Rewrite the general sentences below with more specific details.
Use adjectives, nouns, verbs, and adverbs.

General	With Specific Details
1. He bought a vegetable.	He bought some bright green spinach.
2. We returned from the store.	_____
3. I entered the room.	_____
4. My friend cleaned the spinach.	_____
5. We put the spinach in the pan.	_____
6. Our guests enjoyed the dinner.	_____

Language Focus

Similes

Descriptive writing may use similes to make something seem more familiar or more creative. Similes make ideas easier to understand, and they can also express feelings. Similes are often used in literature and poetry. Look at the famous examples below:

The sun was like a glowing ball of fire.
   —Shakespeare

I was young and easy ... and happy as the grass was green.
   —Dylan Thomas

My love is like a red, red rose.
   —Robert Burns

Simile Structure

• A simile can use the preposition *like* + noun or noun phrase.
   The stars looked **like** underline{diamonds}.

• A simile can also use *as ... as* + noun or noun phrase. This kind of simile also uses an adjective.
   He is **as** clever **as** a fox.

Identifying similes

Match the first half of each sentence with the second half.

_____ 1. The house	a. smelled sweet like honey.
_____ 2. The ocean	b. is as solid as a rock.
_____ 3. The cold wind	c. sparkles like a diamond.
_____ 4. Their friendship	d. was as fast as a bullet.
_____ 5. The train	e. cut sharply like a knife.
_____ 6. The air	f. was as huge as a castle.

Exercise 6 **Writing similes**

Fill in the blanks below to make your own similes with _like_ or _as_.

1. My best friend _____.

2. The place where I grew up _____.

3. My home _____.

4. My favorite music _____.

5. Coffee _____.

6. TV _____.

Exercise 7 **Writing a first draft**

Review your outline. Then write the first draft of a three-paragraph essay on a food you strongly like or dislike.

Exercise 8 **Peer editing a first draft**

After you write your first draft, exchange it with a partner. Answer the questions on the checklist on page 42. You may also write comments or questions on your partner's draft. Then read your partner's comments on your first draft, and revise it as necessary.

Editor's Checklist

Put a check (✓) as appropriate. Write answers in complete sentences in the lines provided.

☐ 1. Does the essay have three paragraphs?

☐ 2. Does the introduction include a hook to get the reader's attention? Does it also include background information?

☐ 3. Does the body paragraph contain enough descriptive details?

☐ 4. What other description do you think the writer could add?

_____

_____

☐ 5. Did the writer use similes to make the writing more descriptive? Are the similes used correctly?

☐ 6. Did the writer give a final opinion in the conclusion?

In Part 4 you will ...

- learn about the use and formation of adjectives.
- learn about adjective order.
- edit your first draft for mistakes.

PART 4

Editing Your Writing

Now that you have written a first draft, it is time to edit. Editing involves making changes to your writing to improve it and correct mistakes.

Language Focus

Using Adjectives in Descriptive Writing

Adjectives are words that describe nouns—people, places, and things. Adjectives appear in different positions in the sentence.

- Adjectives usually come after an article and before a noun.

  We sat in the **roaring** sun.

- Adjectives can also occur after some stative verbs such as *appear, be, become, feel, look, seem*. Use *and* to separate two adjectives that follow a verb. Separate more than two adjectives with commas and the word *and*.

  I was **hungry**.
  He became **thoughtful**.
  He was **sick** and **tired**.
  We were **excited**, **nervous**, and **anxious**.

Exercise 1 **Identifying adjectives**

Read the following sentences. Circle the adjectives and underline the nouns they describe.

1. The beach was quiet and still.

2. Many crabs were walking slowly on the white sand.

3. The traps looked like round cages.

4. There were some small, fragrant fish in the trap.

5. The fishy smell made the crabs hungry.

6. I smelled the strong smell of the dark, oily fish.

7. The meat was white, pinkish and tender.

8. It tasted sweet.

Formation of Adjectives

- Adjectives may be formed from verbs. Many of these adjectives are formed by adding -ing to verbs.

  entertain entertain**ing**   excite exci**ting**
  (an entertaining film)   (an exciting novel)

- The past participles of verbs can function as adjectives.

  break brok**en**   excite excit**ed**
  (a broken arm)   (an excited child)

- Nouns may also function as adjectives when they are used to describe or modify other nouns. They are called noun modifiers.

  A store that sells shoes ⟶ a **shoe** store

Describing Feelings

- Some adjectives ending in -ed and -ing can be used to talk about feelings and emotions, for example, interesting, interested, boring, bored, confusing, confused.

- The adjectives ending in -ed (past participles) describe how people feel about something.

  The **interested** students listened to the story. (= The students felt interest.)

- The adjectives ending in -ing describe the noun that causes the emotion or feeling.

  The students heard an **interesting** story. (= The story caused interest.)

Exercise 2   **Describing feelings**

Circle the correct adjective in each sentence.

1. The movie was very (bored / boring).

2. The audience was very (confused / confusing) by the story.

3. As a student, I found the class very (interested / interesting).

4. The speaker was very (excited / exciting) by the topic.

5. The children were (tired / tiring) by the game.

6. The new tastes were (stimulated / stimulating) to the chef.

Language Focus

Order of Adjectives

Adjectives appear in a particular order, according to their function, as shown below:

Quality / Opinion	Size	Age	Shape	Color	Origin	Material	Purpose/ Kind
interesting	huge	old	round	blue	Mexican	wooden	picnic
boring	small	new	square	white	European	iron	wedding

We put out **huge** plates of **Mexican** food out on the **wooden picnic** table.

My mother had a **beautiful, small, antique, Tahitian pearl** necklace that she wore for special occasions.

Rosa and Pablo bought **gold wedding** rings.

Exercise 3   **Using adjectives in the correct order**

A. Rewrite the sentences placing the adjectives in the correct order.

1. It was a (metal / new / fantastic) sculpture.

   _____

2. They walked down the (old / elegant / marble) staircase.

   _____

3. The museum had (wooden / entrance / beautiful) doors.

   _____

4. There were (blue / huge / bright) lights to mark the entrance.

   _____

5. The food was served in (simple / tiny) portions on (small / dinner / modern) plates.

   _____

6. The women wore (velvet / new / stunning) dresses.

   _____

B. Add two adjectives for each of the sentences.

1. It was a _____, _____ car.
2. They lived in a _____, _____ house.
3. The house was located on a _____, _____ street.
4. She enjoyed the _____, _____ movie.

Editing a paragraph

Read the paragraph and correct the order of the adjectives as necessary. There are eight mistakes.

I love Saturday night dinner at my family's house. We leave at two in the afternoon, and take the drive long to my parents' house. They live on a narrow dirt road. In summer we have to close the windows to the car so that the dust doesn't come in. It is a large, wooden, white house, with a red, old, big door. There is a kitchen spacious where everyone helps prepare the dinner. Everyone in my family gathers for dinner on Saturday night, all my sisters and brothers and their children. The thing I love the most about the house is walking into the dining room after we finish preparing the dinner. The old, beautiful table is set with a lace, white tablecloth and round, huge platters of food. Then everyone sits down in the big, comfortable chairs to enjoy the dinner. We talk and eat for hours and enjoy our family. Everyone feels happy, relaxed and full. Late at night, we finally say goodbye until the next Saturday.

Editing your first draft and rewriting

Review your essay for mistakes. Use the checklist on page 47. Then write a final draft.

Editor's Checklist

Put a check (✓) as appropriate.

- [ ] 1. Did you use adjectives after articles and before nouns?
- [ ] 2. Did you use adjectives immediately after stative verbs?
- [ ] 3. If a sentence has more than one adjective, do the adjectives appear in the correct order?
- [ ] 4. Did you use prepositional phrases to show location and time?

In Part 5 you will …

- review the elements of descriptive writing.
- practice writing with a time limit.

PART 5

Putting It All Together

In this part of the unit, you will complete four exercises to improve your accuracy, write a timed essay to improve your fluency, and explore topics for future writing.

Exercise 1 **Identifying prepositional phrases**

Circle the examples of prepositional phrases.

1. On Saturday we walked to the pizza restaurant in Cabimas.

2. The pizzas that came out of the oven looked delicious.

3. We watched with excitement as the waiter brought the pizza to our table.

3. My favorite pizza comes with sausage and mushrooms on top.

4. The cheese on top of it is hot, and the crust crunches in your mouth when you bite it.

5. There are four chairs around each table.

6. There are a few tables outside the restaurant.

Exercise 2 **Identifying adjectives**

Read the following sentences. Circle the adjectives and underline the nouns they describe.

1. The table was long and narrow.

2. It had tall, straight chairs on each side.

3. It gave the dining room an elegant feeling.

4. Small candles decorated each place.

5. In front of each chair was a delicate lace napkin.

6. Each napkin sat on top of a shiny dinner plate.

7. The guests arrived in beautiful clothing and full of lively conversation.

8. The evening was filled with the warm energy of close friends.

Using adjectives

Rewrite the sentences. For each sentence, use all three adjectives given.

1. The (enormous / wild / exciting) jungle was filled with life.

   _____

2. The (ancient / stone / huge) temples could be seen for miles.

   _____

3. The (gray / tall / rough) steps led to the top.

   _____

4. A (spectacular / vast / green) view could be seen in every direction.

   _____

5. People marveled at the (amazing / ageless / tropical) landscape.

   _____

6. In their amazement, they forgot their (modern / shiny / small) cameras.

   _____

Correcting order of adjectives

**Read the following sentences. If the sentence is correct, write _C._
If the sentence is incorrect, write _I_ and rewrite the sentence correcting
the mistakes.**

_____ 1. The thing I like most about visiting my parents is sleeping in my bed old.

_____ 2. Katerina's baby was small and beautiful.

_____ 3. Sebastian enjoyed the delicious meal gourmet.

_____ 4. They painted the house an antique lovely grey.

_____ 5. There were fourteen people seated in the old dining room.

_____ 6. Montreal is a city with a history rich.

TIMED WRITING: 60 minutes

**Write a three-paragraph descriptive essay on a tradition in your culture.
Before you begin to write, review the following time management
strategy.**

BRAINSTORMING: 5 minutes

Write down ideas and vocabulary for your essay in the box or on a separate piece of paper. You may want to cluster your ideas.

```



```

OUTLINING: 5 minutes

Write an outline for your essay.

Introduction

Hook: _____

_____

_____

_____

Background information: _____

_____

_____

_____

Thesis statement: _____

_____

_____

Body Paragraph

Topic sentence: _____

_____

_____

_____

_____

Descriptive details: _____

_____

_____

_____

Conclusion

_____

_____

_____

Step 3 **WRITING: 40 minutes**

Use your brainstorming notes and outline to write your first draft on a separate piece of paper.

Step 4 **EDITING: 10 minutes**

When you have finished your first draft, check it for mistakes, using the checklist below.

Editor's Checklist

Put a check (✓) as appropriate.

☐ 1. Does the essay have three paragraphs?

☐ 2. Does the introduction include a hook and a thesis?

☐ 3. Does the body paragraph contain enough descriptive details? Do the details support the topic sentence of the body paragraph?

☐ 4. Does the conclusion state a final opinion?

☐ 5. Are adjectives used after articles and before nouns?

☐ 6. Are adjectives used immediately after stative verbs?

☐ 7. Do adjectives appear in correct order?

☐ 8. Did you use prepositional phrases to show location and time?

1. **Write a three-paragraph descriptive essay on one of the following topics.**

   - A holiday celebration or family tradition
   - A particular or favorite place or time of day
   - A work of art (painting, sculpture, photograph, etc.)
   - A piece of architecture (bridge, skyscraper, etc.)

2. **Write a three-paragraph descriptive essay from a friend's point of view.**

   - Select a topic from the list above.
   - Interview a friend about his or her views on the topic.
   - Take notes during the interview
   - Use your notes to write your essay.

3. **Use the Internet or other sources to research one of the topics in item 1 above or a topic of your own choice. Write a descriptive essay based upon your research.**

Narrative Essays

Unit Goals

Rhetorical focus:
- narrative organization

Language focus:
- showing sequence in narrative essays
- adding detail to essays

PART 1

Stimulating Ideas

Formative experiences are experiences that shape how we see the world and what type of person we become later in life. In this unit, you will write a narrative about one such experience.

Thinking about the topic

A. Discuss the pictures with a partner.

- What is happening in the pictures? How do you know?
- What do the pictures have in common?

B. Make notes about three important events or experiences in your life. Then discuss in small groups.

- Describe each event.
- Why was it important?
- How did it change you?

Reading about the topic

U.S. President and humanitarian Jimmy Carter wrote the following narrative passage. It describes his childhood experience "mopping cotton" on his father's farm during the 1930s. To kill insects that ate cotton plants, Carter's family covered each cotton plant with molasses mixed with poison.

Breaking Ground to Be a Man

Mopping cotton was a terrible job. The **molasses** attracted **swarms** of flies and honeybees. They covered the **barrel**, and followed us through the field. I usually wore short pants and never underwear or a shirt during the warm months, but for this job I preferred to protect my legs with long pants. My pants quickly became covered with the poison, and stuck uncomfortably to my legs. In fact, everything about me was sticky. With time, my pants dried, and the sweet, sticky poison turned to hard sugar, so that at night my stiff pants wouldn't fold, but stood up alone in a corner or against the furniture. They were covered with poison, so they had to be washed separately from the other clothing. For this reason, we didn't change them every day. It was terrible to put them back on in the mornings.

Child farm worker, 1930s.

Carter, J. *An Hour Before Daylight*, (Adapted). New York: Simon & Schuster, 2001: 180–181.

molasses: a thick sugar syrup
swarm: a large group that is in motion (usually insects)
barrel: a round wooden container used for storage

Exercise 3   **Understanding the text**

Write *T* for true or *F* for false for each statement.

_____ 1. Carter wore shorts when he mopped cotton.

_____ 2. The poison turned from a liquid to a solid on his pants.

_____ 3. Carter folded his pants every night before he went to sleep.

_____ 4. Carter washed his pants with his other clothes.

Responding to the text

Write your answers for each question in full sentences. Then discuss your answers with a partner.

1. Carter wrote: "I preferred to protect my legs with long trousers." Why was this necessary? _____

   _____

   _____

2. Was this a comfortable job? Why or why not? How do you think Carter felt about it? _____

   _____

   _____

3. Why do you think this was an important formative experience for him?

   _____

   _____

4. Have you ever had a difficult job or task? What was it? _____

   _____

   _____

Freewriting

Write for ten to fifteen minutes on the topic below. Express yourself as well as you can. Don't worry about mistakes.

In the passage, Jimmy Carter describes difficult and uncomfortable work on his parents' farm. On a separate piece of paper, write about a difficult job you have had or task you have done.

- Describe the job or task.
- How did you feel about it?
- What did you learn from it?
- Did this experience change you in any way?

> **In Part 2 you will …**
>
> - learn about narrative organization.
> - brainstorm ideas and specific vocabulary to use in your writing.
> - create an outline for your essay.

Brainstorming and Outlining

✍ WRITING TASK

In this unit, you will write a three-paragraph narrative essay about an important experience that changed you or taught you something important.

Exercise 1 **Brainstorming ideas**

A. Think back to the three events you discussed in Exercise 1B on page 54. Can you add any more events to the list? Choose one of the events to write about in your narrative essay. Use the following questions to help you in your choice.

1. Which of these events had the strongest influence on you?
2. What effects did this event have on your life?
3. Which of these events do you feel comfortable writing about?
4. Which of these events would make the best story?
5. Once you have selected your topic, write it here. _____

_____

B. On a separate sheet of paper, brainstorm a list of details related to this event. Try to expand on your original notes with more detail. Think about who was there; and when, what, and where the event happened.

Exercise 2 **Brainstorming vocabulary**

A. Think about the event. Try to recall your actions and emotions. Add two or three more words to each set.

1. **Actions:** hurry (to), gaze (at), warn (someone), suffer (from), notice (someone / something), _____, _____, _____

2. **Emotions:** nervous, eager, relieved, worried, amazed, confused,

_____, _____, _____

B. Circle words you would like to use from the sets. On a separate piece of paper, practice using these words in sentences. Use your dictionary for help.

Rhetorical Focus

Narrative Organization

A narrative is a story. It has an introduction that engages the reader's interest, a body that gives details about the main event or action in the story, and a conclusion that describes the outcome.

Introduction
- The hook gets the reader's attention.
- The middle sentences introduce an event (the action of the story) by providing background information about the people, the place, and the time.
- The thesis statement prepares the reader for the action that follows.

Body Paragraphs
- The body paragraphs describe what happened in the story.
- They include details that bring the story to life.
- They often use time order to explain the event.

Conclusion
- A conclusion describes the outcome of the event.
- It often ends with a comment by the writer about what the event showed or taught.

Exercise 3   **Reading a student essay**

Read the essay. What was the writer's embarrassing incident?

An Embarrassing Incident

Where I grew up, the rules for family life are very strict. I had five brothers and five sisters, and we spent a lot of time with our relatives. My parents taught us we should respect grandparents more than anyone in the world because grandparents had lived the longest. They had more knowledge about life, and no matter what they said, even if it did not make sense, they were right. We were taught that to hug or kiss grandparents was disrespectful and that we should greet them by kissing their hand. I was young, and I thought that everyone lived and thought just as I did. Well, I soon found out this is not true.

One day, an American friend invited me to her birthday party. I was very excited but at the same time very nervous. I wanted her family to like me, and I wanted to use my best manners. Slowly, I walked up to the house and rang the bell. My friend came running out with a big smile, telling me she was happy that I came. Then she let me in and introduced me to her parents. They smiled and said hello. Later she said, "Come here. I want you to meet my grandpa." I followed her into the living room where her grandfather was sitting. She introduced us, and he reached out his hand. He was going to shake hands, but I thought he was expecting me to kiss his hand, so I did. He pulled his hand away and looked at me in a strange way as if he did not like what I had done. Everyone else in the room looked at me, and my friend started laughing. I was very confused. I sat down and tried to figure out what had happened. Just then, a little boy ran to my friend's grandfather and jumped on his lap. The little boy started to hug and kiss the grandfather. When I saw this, I got up and took the little boy by the hand and said, "NO." I guess I said it pretty loudly because the room became very silent and all eyes were on me.

The next day at school my friend asked me why I kissed her grandfather's hand and why I told the little boy to get away from his grandfather. I explained my customs to her and she explained hers to me. Finally, I learned that good manners are not always the same in different countries. Fortunately, my friend and I stayed very good friends.

Exercise 4   **Analyzing the student essay**

A. **Respond to the essay by answering the questions below in full sentences.**

1. What background information do you learn about the writer? Why is this information important to understand the story? _____

_____

2. What is the main event or action in the story? _____

_____

3. What does the writer learn? _____

_____

B. Examine the organization of the essay by answering the questions below. Then compare your answers with a partner.

1. Underline the hook. Is it one sentence or two? _____

2. Underline the sentences that give background information. What do you learn from this information? _____

   _____

   _____

3. Underline the thesis statement. Is it one sentence or two? _____

4. Reread the body paragraph. Circle one or two details that you like.

5. Circle any words that help you visualize the event more clearly.

6. Reread the conclusion. Underline the sentences that explain what the writer learned.

7. Rewrite the author's conclusion in your own words. _____

   _____

   _____

Exercise 5   **Writing an outline**

Review your brainstorming ideas and your freewriting exercise. Then use the form to write an outline for your essay. Remember to write your outline in note form.

Introduction

Think of a hook that will engage the reader. _____

_____

_____

Think of relevant background information your reader will need to understand the story. _____

_____

_____

_____

Thesis statement: _____

_____

_____

Body Paragraph

Give the events of your narrative in the order in which they happened. Make note of any words connected to the story. _____

_____

_____

_____

_____

_____

_____

Conclusion

What did you learn from the event? _____

_____

_____

_____

_____

In Part 3 you will ...

- learn about showing sequence in a narrative essay.
- learn about adding details to your essay.
- write a first draft of your narrative essay.

PART 3

Developing Your Ideas

Reading a student essay

Read the essay. What is the scary secret?

A Scary Secret

My sister and I made a dangerous mistake one summer. I was thirteen and my sister was fourteen, and our parents had taken us to the city where they grew up. We felt very grown up as we rode to the hotel in a taxi. The hotel was very big, and it had a blue tile floor. After we unpacked our suitcases, our parents wanted to go to the market. My mother told us not to go outside. "We won't," my sister promised, but I knew that she was lying. We had already decided to go out and explore this strange and beautiful city by ourselves.

As soon as my parents were out of sight, we got our things and went downstairs. We walked out of the hotel doors and down a narrow street. The sun was setting, and the light was very beautiful. We could hear the noises of traffic nearby, but the little street was quiet. Suddenly, a man with a gun stepped out from a doorway. He said, "Don't move!" He was short, and he was wearing a dark green jacket and sunglasses. He came very close and we could smell cigarettes and something terrible in his breath. We were terrified and couldn't say anything. He said, "Give me your shoes." So I did. Then he took my sister's purse and her gold ring and ran away. I remember that I fell against my sister. I heard her take a deep breath; she was shaking. Afterward, we ran back to the hotel, across the blue tile floor and up to our room.

The man scared us, but he also taught us something important. Before this experience, we did not always listen to our parents. We now learned that we should obey them. My sister and I became obedient daughters, and we enjoyed the rest of our vacation. However, we decided not to tell our parents about our adventure. We knew they would punish us even though we had learned our lesson. This dangerous adventure is still a secret that I share with my sister.

Exercise 2 **Analyzing the student essay**

Respond to the essay by answering the questions below in full sentences.

1. Underline and label the hook in the introduction. Does it get your attention?

2. Underline and label the thesis statement. What will the body paragraph discuss according to the thesis? _____

   _____

   _____

   _____

3. What events are given in the body paragraph? Which descriptive details make the story vivid, or easy to imagine? _____

   _____

   _____

   _____

4. What was the outcome of the story that is explained in the conclusion? What did the girls learn as a result? _____

   _____

   _____

   _____

Showing Sequence in Narrative Essays

In narrative essays, we use time expressions to make the chronological sequence of events clear.

- We use connectors (time adverbs) such as *then*, *finally*, or *eventually* to link sentences within a paragraph.

- We use subordinating conjunctions to link clauses within a sentence.

Time Adverbs

We use time adverbs such as *afterward, after that, eventually, finally, later, later on, now, then,* and *suddenly* as connectors. These connectors usually appear at the beginning of a sentence. When they do, they are immediately followed by a comma.

⚠ *Then* is an exception. It is not followed by a comma.

Our train was running late. **Finally,** it arrived.
We got on board the train. **Then** we realized that we did not have money for the fare.

Exercise 3   **Identifying time adverbs**

Read the student essay on pages 62–63. Circle the time adverbs. On a separate piece of paper, write sentences of your own using the adverbs you found. After you finish, compare your sentences with a partner.

Language Focus

Subordinating Conjunctions

We use subordinating conjunctions such as *as soon as, before, after, when,* and *while* in complex sentences as connectors. Complex sentences contain a main (independent) clause and a dependent clause.

- The main clause expresses the principal and independent idea of the sentence. The dependent clause expresses additional information about the main idea (for example, where or when it happened) but would be meaningless without the main idea. Dependent time clauses tell us when something happened.

- Subordinating conjunctions establish the time relationship between the dependent time clause and the main clause in the sentence. The subordinating conjunction starts the dependent clause, but the clauses can come in either order. We use a comma when the time clause comes before the main clause.

time clause	main clause
After our parents left the hotel,	we went into the street.
While we were unpacking,	the lights went out.

main clause	time clause
We went into the street	**after** our parents left the hotel.
The lights went out	**while** we were unpacking.

Exercise 4   Using subordinating conjunctions in time clauses

Combine each pair of sentences into one complex sentence. Use the subordinating conjunctions in parentheses to clarify time relationships.

1. We went to the movies. We ate lunch at a restaurant. (after) _____

   _____

2. We waited a long time for the bus. It arrived. (before) _____

   _____

3. They saved enough money. They took a great vacation. (as soon as) _____

   _____

4. She thought carefully about which dress to buy. She bought the
   red one. (before) _____

   _____

5. I listened to the radio. I prepared dinner. (while) _____

   _____

6. She worked very hard for many years. She retired. (then) _____

   _____

7. I was very surprised. You knocked on my door. (when) _____

   _____

8. He had a cup of coffee. He got up in the morning. (as soon as) _____

   _____

Language Focus

Adding Details to Essays

Details are facts, examples, illustrations, definitions, and descriptions that make ideas or events clear. They answer *who, what, why, where, when,* and *how* questions. We add details to make our writing clearer and more effective.

General		Detail
He went on vacation.	*Why?*	Because he was completely exhausted.
	How?	He saved his money for a plane ticket.
	Where?	He traveled to Africa.
	Who?	Although he traveled alone, he met many interesting people.

Exercise 5   Asking detail questions about an outline

Look at this outline and help the writer generate details by writing questions using *who, what, where, why,* or *how.*

The Day I Became a Hero

Hook: When I was eleven, I learned an important lesson about myself in gym class.

1. Questions: <u>What exactly did you learn? Where did you learn it?</u>
   <u>Who were you with? How did you learn it?</u>

Thesis statement: All the girls were afraid to jump over the pommel horse, but I was tired of waiting, so I decided to try.

2. Questions: _____

   _____

Topic sentence: I decided I wanted to go first.

3. Questions: _____

   _____

Supporting detail: I was overjoyed. I had jumped over the pommel horse without falling down.

4. Questions: _____

   _____

Conclusion: That day, I learned that I like to do things that are a little bit hard.

5. Questions: _____

   _____

Exercise 6 Adding details to your outline

Give the outline for your essay to a partner and have him or her write
questions about it for you.

Exercise 7 Writing a first draft

Review your outline. Look at your partner's questions about your
outline. Then write the first draft of a three-paragraph essay about a
learning experience that changed you or taught you something valuable.

Exercise 8 Peer editing a first draft

After you write your first draft, exchange it with a partner. Answer the
questions on the checklist below. You may also write comments or
questions on your partner's draft. Then read your partner's comments
on your first draft, and revise it as necessary.

Editor's Checklist

Put a check (✓) as appropriate.

- [ ] 1. Does the introduction include a hook to get the reader's attention and background information?
- [ ] 2. Does the introduction have a thesis statement that briefly describes the action that will follow?
- [ ] 3. Does the body paragraph have a clear topic sentence?
- [ ] 4. Does the body paragraph include details that explain the events? Which is the most interesting detail?
- [ ] 5. Does the essay include time expressions, such as time adverbs and subordinating conjunctions?
- [ ] 6. Does the conclusion explain the outcome, or what you learned from the experience?

In Part 4 you will ...

- review the past continuous.
- learn about past time clauses.
- edit your first draft.
- write a second draft.

PART 4

Editing Your Writing

Now that you have written a first draft, it is time to edit. Editing involves making changes to your writing to improve it and correct mistakes.

Language Focus

Using the Past Continuous in Narrative Essays

In a narrative, you often need to describe actions in progress, or to describe background actions.

- To form the past continuous use *was/were* and the base form of the verb + *ing*.

- Use the past continuous to talk about activities that were in progress at a specific time in the past. The activities began before the specific time and may also have continued after that time.

  At three o'clock we **were walking** home from school. My friend **was riding** his bicycle.

- Also use the past continuous to describe background actions.

  The sun **was going** down and the children **were** still **playing** on the grass.

⚠ We don't usually use stative verbs (*be, know, own, mean, seem, understand, love, believe*, etc.) in the past continuous. We use the simple past instead.

  I **didn't know** John then.
  I wasn't knowing John then. (INCORRECT)

Affirmative Statements		
SUBJECT	*WAS/WERE*	VERB + *ING*
I	was	working.
They	were	
The sun	was	shining.

Negative Statements		
SUBJECT	*WAS/WERE + NOT*	VERB + *ING*
She	wasn't	working .
We	weren't	
The phone	wasn't	ringing.

Identifying background action

Read the paragraph below and underline all the verbs that describe
background actions.

My Wedding

I will always remember my wedding day. It was beautiful. I woke up
and looked outside. The sun was shining, and the birds were singing.
It was as if they were talking to me, telling me to get up. In reality, the
circle radio was playing and my brothers were arguing in the hallway,
but it still felt romantic. My dress was hanging on the closet door.
My mother was cooking breakfast in the kitchen, and the coffee was
brewing. My father was talking on the phone to his brother, and they
were discussing who was the better chess player. This was a constant
argument between the two of them, but I knew my father was just
trying to distract himself because he was feeling nervous.

Using the past continuous to describe actions in progress

Complete the following sentences using the past continuous.

1. I'm sorry I wasn't home yesterday afternoon, _I was walking my dog in_
   the park .

2. When my uncle visited in 2004, I _____.

3. Last week was very busy, my roommate and I had many tests and
   assignments to complete. While I _____,
   she _____.

4. I'm sorry I couldn't talk last night. When you called, we _____.
   _____.

5. I'm so tired! Last night, my sister and I _____ until
   two in the morning!

6. I didn't hear the doorbell. The radio _____ too loudly.

Setting the scene with background details

> Continue the stories below. Give background actions using the
> past continuous to help set the scene. Use the sample paragraph in
> Exercise 1 as a model.

1. It was an ordinary day at school. _____
   _____
   _____
   _____
   _____
   _____
   _____
   _____. Suddenly, the fire alarm went off.

2. It was a cold and rainy night. _____
   _____
   _____
   _____
   _____
   _____
   _____
   _____. And then someone knocked at the door.

Language Focus

Past Time Clauses

Past time clauses can be used to describe the relationship between two
or more events.

- Past time clauses are dependent clauses. They must be attached to a
  main (or independent) clause.

- Past time clauses can contain verbs in the past continuous or simple
  past, and usually begin with subordinating conjunctions such as
  before, when, while, and *after.*

- The past time clause can come before or after the main clause;
  however, if the past time clause comes first, separate it from the main
  clause with a comma.

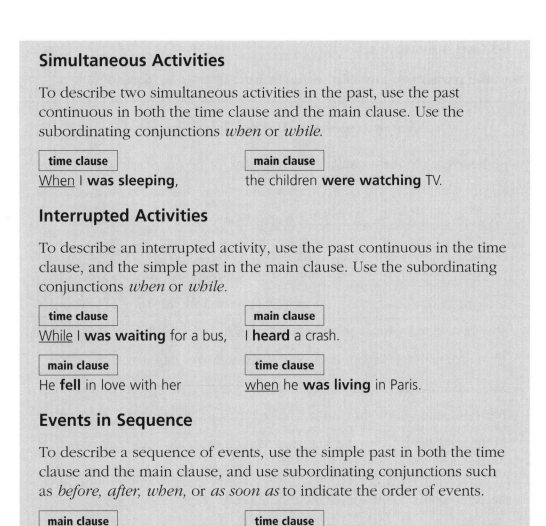

Simultaneous Activities

To describe two simultaneous activities in the past, use the past continuous in both the time clause and the main clause. Use the subordinating conjunctions *when* or *while*.

time clause	main clause
When I **was sleeping**,	the children **were watching** TV.

Interrupted Activities

To describe an interrupted activity, use the past continuous in the time clause, and the simple past in the main clause. Use the subordinating conjunctions *when* or *while*.

time clause	main clause
While I **was waiting** for a bus,	I **heard** a crash.

main clause	time clause
He **fell** in love with her	when he **was living** in Paris.

Events in Sequence

To describe a sequence of events, use the simple past in both the time clause and the main clause, and use subordinating conjunctions such as *before, after, when,* or *as soon as* to indicate the order of events.

main clause	time clause
I walked past my sister	**before** I recognized her.

time clause	main clause
As soon as I heard the news,	I ran into the street to tell my friends.

Exercise 4   **Practicing time clauses**

Read the following sentences. Write *S* (simultaneous) if the sentence involves two simultaneous actions. Write *I* (interrupted) if the sentence involves one action interrupting another. Write *SQ* (sequence) if the sentence involves two actions happening in sequence.

_____ 1. My dog was eating its dinner while my cat was playing with a toy.

_____ 2. We learned to read the alphabet before we learned to write the letters.

_____ 3. After we saw the movie, we went out for a hamburger.

_____ 4. Petra was flying into the airport while her daughter was having a baby.

_____ 5. Aaron called Veronica as soon as he saw Jacob.

_____ 6. Martin was sleeping when he received the call.

Editing a paragraph

Read the paragraph and edit as necessary. There are nine mistakes.

My Vacation in the Mountains

People go to the mountains on vacation for two reasons: to ski and to enjoy the view. My family doesn't ski but we wanted to enjoy the view! In pictures, the mountains were always beautiful. The flowers were blooming, the sun was shining, and the people were smiling; however, our trip to the mountains was a disaster. As soon as we were arriving at our destination, the sun disappeared. It was rain. I We were stay in a friend's small apartment. My father went to the window in the living room every day and checked the sky. Every day it was the same: rainy and cloudy. One day, while he was look at the clouds, a little sun began to shine through. He saw the sun as soon as, we were jumping in the car. We drove to the Jungfrau Mountain so we could take the tram to the top and enjoy the view. We eagerly got on the tram. It began to climb to the top of the mountain. However, while the tram was climbing, it becoming cloudy. The tram arrived at the top of the mountain, and we got out. We were in the middle of a cloud. I thought it was exciting, but my father didn't. We drove back in silence. Our last day we went to the airport and then were getting on the plane. Just as the plane was taking off, the sun was beginning to shine again.

Editing your first draft and rewriting

Review your essay for mistakes. Use the checklist on page 73. Then write a final draft.

Editor's Checklist

Put a check (✓) as appropriate.

☐ 1. Did you use the correct verb forms for sequence, interruption, and simultaneous actions?

☐ 2. Did you check that stative verbs were used in the past simple only?

☐ 3. Does the essay include time expressions such as time adverbs and subordinating conjunctions?

In Part 5 you will …

- review time adverbs and subordinating conjunctions.
- review the simple past and the past continuous.
- write a timed narrative essay.

PART 5

Putting It All Together

In this part of the unit, you will complete three exercises to improve your accuracy, write a timed essay to improve your fluency, and explore topics for future writing.

| Exercise 1 | **Using time adverbs and subordinating conjunctions** |

Rewrite the sentence(s) as either one or two correctly punctuated sentences. Use the words in parentheses.

1. The day of my brother's birthday was very exciting first we went to the store to buy all the ingredients we came home and prepared the food for the party. (then)

   _____

   _____

   _____

2. We went to the store to buy all the ingredients. We came home and prepared the food for the party. (before)

   _____

   _____

3. In the beginning, writing was difficult it is easier. (now)

   _____

4. Writing became easier for him. He started doing it more frequently. (after)

   _____

5. When I was a child, I used to think I would never learn to play baseball, but I was wrong I became good at it. (eventually)

   _____

   _____

6. I used to think I would never learn how to play baseball. I was a child. (when)

   _____

   _____

7. I never enjoyed eating vegetables when I was young I started to like the taste. (later on)

   _____

   _____

8. I was young. I never enjoyed eating vegetables. (when)

   _____

9. I was afraid of the water until we moved to a house near a lake I learned
   how to swim. (after that)

   _____

   _____

10. I wasn't afraid of the water. I learned how to swim. (as soon as)

    _____

11. The movie was long and boring. Sebastian thought it would never end it
    did. (finally)

    _____

    _____

12. Sebastian was watching the long and boring movie. He had the feeling that
    it would never end. (while)

    _____

    _____

Exercise 2   Reviewing the simple past and past continuous

Write the correct form of the verbs in parentheses.

Last Saturday was an exciting day for me. It was my birthday. I
worked until eight o'clock as usual. As I _____ (walk) to
the bus stop, I _____ (look) for my younger brother. But
that day he wasn't there. I _____ (think) it was strange,
but I _____ (imagine) he was out with his friends. When
I _____ (arrive) at my house, I _____
(notice) all the lights were turned off. While I _____
(look for) my front door keys, I _____ (hear) a noise
and suddenly all the lights came on. All my friends and family were in
my house. When I opened the door, they all yelled, "Surprise!" It was a
surprise birthday party for me, and I never suspected a thing!

Read the paragraph and edit as necessary. There are six mistakes.

Stranger on a Bus

One morning I was wait at the bus stop. I was worried about being late for school, and I was anxiously waiting for the bus to arrive. It was late as usual, and I began to think of what I would tell my teacher. There were several people at the bus stop, and some of them were complaining. When the bus finally came, we all pushed our way on board. Someone folded his umbrella and sprayed water on me. I was felt upset, but fortunately, I got a place next to the window. I had a good view of the sidewalk. People was hurrying along clutching their umbrellas. Then a boy on a bike caught my attention. He was riding beside the bus and wave his arms. I heard passengers behind me shouting to the bus driver, but he refused to stop until we reached the next bus stop. Still, the boy kept riding. He was carried something over his shoulder and shouting. Finally, when we came to the next stop, the boy was running up to the door. I heard an excited conversation. Then the bus driver stood up and announced, "Did anyone lose a briefcase at the last stop?" A woman at the back of the bus, shouted, "Oh my! It's mine." She pushed her way to the front and gratefully took the briefcase. She thanked the little boy with enthusiasm. After that, everyone on the bus began talking about what the boy had done, and the crowd of strangers suddenly became friendly.

 TIMED WRITING: 60 minutes

Write a three-paragraph narrative essay on a formative experience from your past. Before you begin to write, review the following time management strategy.

Step 1   **BRAINSTORMING: 5 minutes**

Write down ideas and vocabulary for your essay on a separate piece of paper. You may want to cluster your ideas.

OUTLINING: 5 minutes

Write an outline for your essay.

Introduction

Hook: _____

_____

_____

Background information: _____

_____

_____

Thesis statement: _____

_____

_____

Body

Topic sentence: _____

_____

_____

Descriptive details: _____

_____

_____

Conclusion

_____

_____

WRITING: 40 minutes

Use your brainstorming notes and outline to write your essay on a separate piece of paper. As you write, remember to include specific details about the experience.

EDITING: 10 minutes

When you have finished your essay, check it for mistakes using the checklist on page 78.

Editor's Checklist

Put a check (✓) as appropriate.

☐ 1. Does the essay have three paragraphs?

☐ 2. Does the introduction include a hook and a thesis?

☐ 3. Does the body paragraph contain enough background information and specific details? Do they support the topic sentence of the body paragraph?

☐ 4. Does the essay include time adverbs and subordinating conjunctions?

☐ 5. Are all the verbs in the correct form?

☐ 6. Does the conclusion explain what you learned from the experience?

Topics for Future Writing

1. **Write a three-paragraph essay on one of the following topics.**

   - A special gift I gave or received
   - The first time I met someone who became important to me
   - A favorite childhood memory
   - A mistake that taught me an important lesson
   - A difficult decision I had to make

2. **Write a three-paragraph essay on one of the topics above, but from a friend's point of view. Interview a friend, classmate, or relative about his or her views on the topic. Take notes during the interview to use for your essay.**

3 **Use the Internet or other sources to research one of the topics or a topic of your choice, then write a three-paragraph essay on the topic.**

Opinion Essays

Unit Goals

Rhetorical focus:
- opinion organization
- facts and opinions
- counter-argument and refutation

Language focus:
- using quantity expressions in opinion essays
- using connectors to show support and opposition

PART 1

Stimulating Ideas

Some people like change while others prefer traditional ways of living and doing things. In this unit, you will choose a recent invention or discovery and write an opinion paper discussing why you think it is beneficial or harmful to society.

Exercise 1   Thinking about the topic

A. Discuss the picture with a partner.

- Describe the picture.
- Where is the man?
- What is he doing?
- In what ways do you think his life is different from the life his parents lived as children?

B. Make notes about the changes in the way we live that have occurred in the past century. Then discuss in small groups.

Exercise 2   Reading about the topic

This article discusses a project to bring wireless communication to Bhutan, a country high in the mountains of Asia that has a traditional way of life.

Wireless: Bhutan's Hills Are Alive with Sound of Cell Phones

The **ancient** way of life continues in the Himalayan Kingdom of Bhutan. Thimpu, home to the royal family and the government, may be the world's only capital city without traffic lights. But while Bhutan may get by without traffic lights, it has realized it cannot miss out on the **digital revolution**. Soon, thousands of cell phones may ring across the mountain kingdom.

Engineers are traveling across the country, setting up **rural** telecommunications systems. This project will connect the Bhutanese with each other and the outside world through voice and Internet technology. The mountain landscape limits the technology that can be used, so **wireless** is the best solution.

For the engineers, it is a challenging project. Teams bringing equipment will face long pony rides through the mountains. Some villages are so far away that it can take four days to walk there from the nearest road. There are no trains or flights. Engineers also could get sick in the high mountains where some villages are above 3,600 meters (12,000 feet).

For the Bhutanese, this will bring important benefits, such as **distance learning** and **tele-medicine**. "The project is a big change in terms of education and communication for the rural people," said a Bhutanese official. In the villages, people are hoping they can benefit from that kind of access to technology without making too many changes to their ancient way of life.

Curnow, R. "Wireless: Bhutan's hills are alive with sound of cell phones" (Adapted). *The International Herald Tribune:* December 20, 2004.

ancient: very old
digital revolution: a big change that happens to a society with the introduction of digital technology
rural: in the countryside or having to do with life far from big cities
wireless: without wires or cables
distance learning: learning through e-mail and the Internet
tele-medicine: medical care in which a doctor works with patients using telecommunications rather than person-to-person contact

Understanding the text

Write *T* for true or *F* for false for each statement.

_____ 1. The Bhutanese capital is not a typical modern city.

_____ 2. The mountainous landscape of Bhutan limits the kind of technology that can be used there.

_____ 3. Engineers will have an easy time building communications systems in Bhutan.

_____ 4. Wireless technology will probably change the lives of rural Bhutanese people.

Responding to the text

Write your answers to each question in full sentences. Then discuss your answers with a partner.

1. What technological changes have occurred in the past fifty years?

_____

_____

_____

2. Which of these changes have had the biggest effect on everyday life?

_____

_____

_____

3. What were the benefits and/or disadvantages of these changes?

_____

_____

_____

4. What change do you especially like or dislike?

_____

_____

_____

Write for ten to fifteen minutes on the topic below. Express yourself as well you can. Don't worry about mistakes.

The article describes how wireless technology is changing the lives of the Bhutanese people. On a separate piece of paper, write about a specific invention that has changed your life.

- What is the invention?
- How has it changed you or the way you do things?
- Who else has been affected by this invention?
- How do you feel about these changes?

In Part 2 you will …

- learn about opinion organization.
- brainstorm ideas and specific vocabulary to use in your writing.
- create an outline for your essay.

Brainstorming and Outlining

✏️ WRITING TASK

In this unit, you will write a three-paragraph opinion essay about an important invention or discovery that has taken place in your lifetime.

Exercise 1 Brainstorming ideas

A. Read the opinions presented in the charts below. Think of arguments for and against these opinions, and make notes in the *Agree* or *Disagree* columns. Consider your arguments: do you agree or disagree with the opinion? Compare your answers with a partner.

1.

Agree	Opinion	Disagree
	TV is bad for children.	

2.

Agree	Opinion	Disagree
	Space exploration is important and should be funded by the government.	

B. Choose an important invention or discovery that you think has had an important impact on society. Write your opinion about the invention in the middle column. Write arguments that agree with your opinion on the left. Write arguments that disagree with your opinion on the right.

Agree	Opinion (of a discovery or invention)	Disagree

Brainstorming vocabulary

A. Circle the words you would like to use. Add two more words to each set.

1. **Positive changes:** foster, support, encourage, _____, _____

2. **Negative changes:** hinder, discourage, prevent, _____, _____

3. **Relationships:** influence, alter, react (to), _____, _____

4. **Results:** produce, result in, bring about, _____, _____

B. On a separate piece of paper, practice using these words in sentences. Use your dictionary for help.

Rhetorical Focus

Opinion Organization

In an opinion essay, the writer tries to convince the reader of a point of view on a controversial issue (something that people disagree about).

Introduction
- The hook introduces a controversial issue.
- The hook may be a short story or an anecdote, a question, or a surprising statement or fact that makes the reader want to know more.
- The middle sentences explain why the issue is important by giving background information. This background information explains the issue with details about the history or the people involved, what they want, or how it affects them.
- The thesis statement at the end presents the writer's point of view.

Body Paragraph
- The topic sentence has a controlling idea that supports the writer's main argument in the thesis.
- The following sentences support the topic sentence with reasons, facts, and explanations to help the reader understand the writer's point of view.
- The body paragraph often includes a statement that describes the opposing opinion. This is called the counter-argument. The writer then argues against the counter-argument. This is called a refutation. In the refutation, the writer points out weaknesses in the counter-argument, and shows how his own argument is stronger.

Conclusion
- This restates the writer's opinion, but often using different, more persuasive language.
- It may also offer a warning, a prediction, or other type of comment that reinforces the writer's viewpoint.

Read the essay. Does the writer support space exploration?

What Can Space Exploration Do for Me?

Whether we realize it or not, space exploration has changed our lives in dramatic ways. People have walked on the moon, and robots have traveled to Mars. These exciting events have created history, but they are also important because they have provided many practical benefits for humans here on earth.

The importance of space programs can be seen in the technology we use every day. Satellite technology allows people to watch TV shows and listen to radio programs from everywhere on earth. Also, many of the advances in computer technology were first invented to support space exploration. For example, the National Aeronautics and Space Administration (NASA) has contributed to the creation of software that people use every day in manufacturing and design. Robotic technology is another famous example. Engineers designed robots to work on the International Space Station, but now robots are being developed to do jobs here on Earth. Even with all these advances, some people say that space exploration is an expensive luxury that takes money away from important programs such as health care and education. However, if they considered how space technology has improved life on Earth, they would see that space exploration is actually important to civilization.

Space exploration creates a need for technological advances. Later, these advances are used in other ways that help people. Wonderful new inventions such as satellites and computers are just a beginning. In the future, space exploration will provide useful and amazing new inventions that we cannot even imagine in the present.

Examining the student essay

A. Respond to the essay by answering the questions below in full sentences.

1. Would the writer agree with someone who said the space program does not help ordinary people? Why or why not? _____

_____

2. What are some of the benefits that space exploration has produced? _____

_____

3. Why do so many technological advances come from space exploration and not other industries? _____

_____

4. According to the writer, what is the opinion of people who do not support space exploration? _____

_____

_____

B. Examine the organization of the essay by answering the questions below. Then compare your answers with a partner.

1. What strategy does the writer use to hook the reader's attention?
   a. a surprising statement
   b. a story
   c. a question
2. Circle the background information that the writer provides.
3. Which of the following best summarizes the author's thesis statement?
   a. Space exploration creates history.
   b. Space exploration has improved daily life on earth.
   c. Scientists discover many things by accident.
   d. The technology needed for space exploration can be used in other ways.
4. Underline the topic sentence of the body paragraph.
5. Underline examples that support the topic sentence.
6. Do all the supporting sentences relate to the topic sentence? _____
7. Do the examples include facts and explanations? _____
8. Write the counter-argument in your own words. _____

_____

_____

Writing an outline

Review your brainstorming ideas and your freewriting exercise. Then use the chart on page 88 to write an outline for your essay. Remember to write your outline in note form.

Introduction

Hook: _____

_____

_____

Background information: _____

_____

_____

Thesis statement: _____

_____

_____

Body Paragraph

Topic sentence: _____

_____

_____

Examples/reasons: _____

_____

_____

_____

Counter-argument: _____

_____

_____

Refutation: _____

_____

_____

Conclusion

Summary and comment: _____

_____

_____

In Part 3 you will …

- learn to use facts and opinions to support your argument.
- learn about counter-arguments and refutation.
- write a first draft of your opinion essay.

Reading a student essay

Read the essay. What is the best medicine?

The Best Medicine

Last week, I noticed that my son had a bad cold. I took him to the pediatrician, and she told me he had an infection. Then she gave me a prescription for antibiotics. After two days, my son was happy and healthy thanks to this important medicine. Every day doctors prescribe antibiotics to help thousands of patients around the world fight infections. I do not like to think about what might happen if we did not have antibiotics.

Antibiotics are one of the greatest medical inventions in human history for several reasons. First, infections are frequent. Almost everyone has experienced an ear infection or a sinus infection. These common illnesses cause pain and discomfort to millions of people around the world every year. In addition, infections can be life-threatening. For example, sepsis, a dangerous infection of the blood, is responsible for one out of every one hundred hospitalizations. The victims are usually very young, old, or weak. Another reason why antibiotics are important is that they stop an infection from spreading to others. Infectious diseases can quickly travel from person to person if they are not treated right away. Antibiotics are the most effective way to control the spread of these serious illnesses. Recently, many people have argued that doctors prescribe antibiotics too often and that the bacteria that cause infections are becoming stronger as a result. This may be true; however, this evidence does not mean that antibiotics are not important. It simply shows that we must learn to use them wisely.

Infections can attack anyone at any time. They can also attack entire populations. While many infections create minor discomfort and suffering, some are quite dangerous. Antibiotics are the most effective way to treat infections. Without antibiotics, many more people would get seriously ill, and others would die.

Exercise 2   Analyzing the student essay

Respond to the essay by answering the questions below.

1. Underline the hook. Which of the following strategies is used? Circle one.
   a. a story
   b. a fact
   c. a surprising statement
   d. a question

2. Circle the sentence that gives background information.

3. Circle the thesis statement. Does it tell you the writer's position?

4. Underline the topic sentence of the body paragraph.

5. How many main reasons does the writer give in the body paragraph? _____

6. Does the writer introduce a counter-argument? _____

7. Which of the following strategies does the writer use in the conclusion?
   a. giving a warning
   b. making a prediction

Rhetorical Focus

Facts and Opinions

Writers use both facts and opinions to support their position or argument. They state their opinion and then back it up with facts. The difference between facts and opinions is shown below.

- **Fact:** a truth that is scientifically proven or generally accepted
  Antibiotics cure infections.

- **Opinion:** one point of view among many
  Antibiotics are the most important invention of the twentieth century.

Distinguishing facts and opinions

Write *F* if the statement is a fact and *O* if it is an opinion.

_____ 1. Small airplanes are used in advertising.

_____ 2. The modern disposable diaper has dramatically improved
parents' lives.

_____ 3. Many nations are working together to build and maintain the
International Space Station.

_____ 4. Internet dating services offer an excellent way to find a husband or
a wife.

_____ 5. Online courses are easier than classroom courses.

Rhetorical Focus

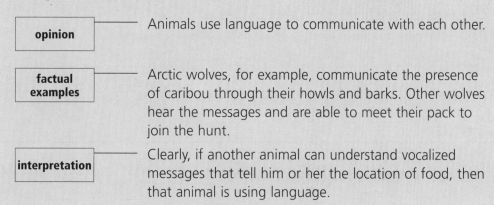

Interpreting Facts to Support an Opinion

After the writer gives factual examples, she or he then interprets the
facts, explaining how they support her or his opinion. Look at the
example below, which includes an opinion, factual examples, and an
interpretation of the facts.

opinion	Animals use language to communicate with each other.
factual examples	Arctic wolves, for example, communicate the presence of caribou through their howls and barks. Other wolves hear the messages and are able to meet their pack to join the hunt.
interpretation	Clearly, if another animal can understand vocalized messages that tell him or her the location of food, then that animal is using language.

Exercise 4 **Interpreting facts to support opinions**

Read each opinion and fact below. Then write a sentence interpreting
the fact to support the opinion. The first one has been done for you.

1. **Opinion:** The Internet takes too much time away from family life.
   Fact: The average adult in the United States spends six hours per week on
   the Internet.

   Those six hours could be spent doing family activities, such as gardening,
   helping children with homework, or playing games.

2. **Opinion:** The government is doing an excellent job of protecting athletes from the pressure to use performance-enhancing drugs.
   Fact: Athletes are routinely tested for drug use.

   _____

   _____

3. **Opinion:** Employers place too much emphasis on personal appearance.
   Fact: According to a recent study, people with average appearance earn 3 to 8 percent less money than those who are considered beautiful.

   _____

   _____

4. **Opinion:** The cell phone industry is a good place to invest money.
   Fact: One out of every six people owns a cell phone.

   _____

   _____

5. **Opinion:** People spend too much money on food.
   Fact: Americans eat meals outside the home an average of five times per week.

   _____

   _____

6. **Opinion:** People in the United States love pets.
   Fact: Americans spend 5.4 million dollars each year on pets.

   _____

   _____

Rhetorical Focus

Counter-Argument and Refutation

In order to make an opinion essay as persuasive as possible, the writer includes a counter-argument and a refutation.

- The counter-argument is the opposing opinion. It disagrees with the writer's position. By including the counter-argument, the writer shows an understanding of other points of view.

- The refutation is the writer's response to the counter-argument. In the refutation, the writer shows why the counter-argument is weak and the writer's position is strong. The refutation may also address doubts the reader may have about the writer's position.

Look at the example below.

counter-argument	Many people think that a child is unhappy without brothers or sisters; however, most only children would disagree with this statement.
refutation	An only child receives more attention from parents, gets into fewer fights, and has plenty of social contact with friends and classmates.

In the above example, the writer raises a counter-argument (that people think children are unhappy without siblings). Then the writer gives a refutation: only children are not unhappy, and then gives reasons to support the argument.

Exercise 5 Recognizing counter-arguments and refutations

Read each statement below. Underline the counter-argument. Circle the writer's refutation.

1. Even though many photographers love film and say they will never give it up, digital cameras are the cameras of the future.

2. Train travel may be inexpensive and relaxing; however, airplanes are a much more important means of transportation because they are fast and efficient.

3. Most people agree that a traditional home-cooked meal is best, but they have to admit that convenience and low cost is making fast food more popular with students.

4. While some people believe that online courses will never be as popular as traditional classrooms; technology, cost, and convenience are increasing the demand for online instruction.

5. Some people criticize credit cards for causing debt; however, it is the irresponsibility of consumers, not credit cards, that causes credit card debt.

6. People often comment that technology makes life easier, but in reality, technology only makes it possible for people to do more work in less time.

Exercise 6 Writing a first draft

Review your outline. Then write the first draft of a three-paragraph essay on an invention or discovery that happened in your lifetime.

After you write your first draft, exchange it with a partner. Answer the questions on the checklist. You may also write comments or questions on your partner's draft. Then read your partner's comments on your first draft, and revise it as necessary.

Editor's Checklist

Put a check (✓) as appropriate. Write answers in complete sentences in the lines provided.

☐ 1. Does the essay have three paragraphs?

☐ 2. Does the introduction include a hook to get the reader's attention along with background information?

☐ 3. Is the writer's opinion about the issue clearly stated in the thesis statement?

☐ 4. Does the body paragraph contain facts and reasons that support the opinion?

☐ 5. Put a check in the margin next to the points that you understand and agree with. Explain why you agree. _____

_____

_____

☐ 6. Write one or two questions about something that needs clarification or additional support. _____

_____

_____

In Part 4 you will …

• learn about using quantity expressions.
• learn about overgeneralizations.
• learn to use connectors to show support and opposition.

PART 4

Editing Your Writing

Now that you have written a first draft, it is time to edit. Editing involves making changes to your writing to improve it and correct mistakes.

Language Focus

Using Quantity Expressions in Opinion Essays

In an opinion essay, writers often make general statements about a group or category. It is important to avoid making a statement that is true for some, but not for all members of a group or category. This is called an overgeneralization. Compare the following statements.

Cats hate water.
Most cats hate water.

The first statement suggests that all cats in the world hate water. It is untrue because some cats, such as tigers, are good swimmers and enjoy being in water. In the second statement, the writer uses the quantity expression *most*. The quantity expression qualifies, or limits the generalization, so that the statement is true.

Quantity Expressions

The following patterns guide the use of quantity expressions:

- *Most, a lot of,* and *some* are used with both plural count nouns and noncount nouns.

  Most dormitories have Internet access.
  Some cafeterias offer healthy alternatives to traditional student food.

- *Much* and *a little* are used with noncount nouns. (*Much* is not usually used in affirmative statements. Use *a lot of* instead.)

  Some people have **a lot of** intelligence, but they do not have **much** common sense.
  Students might have **a little** money left for entertainment after paying expenses.

- *Many, several,* and *a few* are used with plural nouns.

  Many Web sites charge a fee for information.
  A few uncooperative participants can destroy a meeting.

Identifying correct quantity expressions

Circle the correct quantity expression in each sentences.

1. (Many / A lot of) creativity is necessary for certain types of technology jobs.

2. There are (a few / a little) places where the sea level is rising.

3. (A little / Several) bills in Congress have tried to protect Internet users from fraud.

4. In the history of the Internet, only (a little / a few) computer viruses have created serious damage.

5. (Many / A lot of) time is spent doing research on cures for cancer.

6. Did you know that (a little /a few) sleep-deprivation can harm a person's judgment?

Avoiding overgeneralizations

Using quantity expressions, rewrite the sentences below so that they become more appropriate generalizations.

	Overgeneralization	Appropriate Generalization
1.	Everybody has a TV.	Most people have a TV.
2.	People do not like change.	Many people do not like change.
3.	Computers have the latest software.	
4.	Schools are now wireless.	
5.	Medications have side effects.	
6.	New Yorkers love their city.	
7.	Asian countries have hot and humid climates.	
8.	Pollution affects everything.	

Using Connectors to Show Support and Opposition

When we explain an opinion, we can use connectors to clarify the relationship between ideas. Connectors can be used to signal that the second idea will support the first in some way. They can also be used to contrast the first idea with an opposite or very different idea. When they introduce an independent clause, the connector is followed by a comma.

Connectors That Show Support

- One way to support an idea is to give an example that illustrates the idea. Connectors like *for example* and *in particular* introduce examples.

  Most people are willing to spend money to make their lives easier; **for example,** nearly every new house has an automatic garage door opener.

  Children should avoid junk food; **in particular**, they should stay away from sugary snacks.

- A second way to show support is to add facts or explanations that clarify the idea.

  The automobile industry is responding to consumer demands for more fuel-efficient cars; **in fact,** the number of available models has tripled in the past three years.

Connectors That Show Opposition

It is sometimes difficult for the writer to show that two ideas are opposed to each other. Connectors like *however, in contrast, on the other hand* help the writer focus the reader's attention on differences.

I'm late every morning; **however,** I never get into trouble.

Many people enjoy listening to CDs; **in contrast,** live concerts are more exciting.

Understanding connectors

Each of the sentences below has two clauses joined by a connector.
Write *O* for opposition if the clauses show opposing information and
S for support if they show supporting information, such as an example
or a similar idea.

O 1. The Western calendar is used around the world; however, many
      countries have a traditional calendar that they also use.

___ 2. Most people say they want to exercise; however, only one in ten adults
      works out three times a week or more.

___ 3. Frank Lloyd Wright was an architect who liked straight lines; in
      contrast, Antonio Gaudi preferred bends and curves in his designs.

___ 4. Surgeons try hard to protect their hands; for example, they avoid
      sports such as baseball that might cause an injury to their fingers.

___ 5. The place where I grew up only has two seasons; however, my new
      home, New York, has four.

___ 6. Women often buy a house before getting married; in fact, single
      women purchase approximately one in five homes.

Editing a paragraph

Read the paragraph and edit as necessary. There are four mistakes.

> Most working people will agree that traffic congestion creates
> too much stress. As large cities grow even bigger, there is often so
> many traffic that people's productivity is reduced. There are two good
> solutions that could greatly improve traffic conditions in this city. First,
> high occupancy vehicle lanes (HOV lanes) are effective. A vehicle
> can drive in an HOV lane only if the car has at least two passengers.
> Much workers must begin at work at 9:00 every day, so it is easy for
> them to carpool. If four people ride together, there are three fewer
> cars on the road. Providing affordable public transportation is another
> good solution. Much people like to use public transportation because
> it is cheap and convenient. However, building an effective public
> transportation system costs much money.

Editing your first draft and rewriting

Review your essay for mistakes. Use the checklist below. Then write a final draft.

Editor's Checklist

Put a check (✓) as appropriate.

- ☐ 1. Did you use expressions of quantity?
- ☐ 2. Did you use connectors to show opposition?
- ☐ 3. Did you use connectors to show support?

In Part 5 you will …

- review the elements of opinion writing.
- write a timed opinion essay.

PART 5

Putting It All Together

In this part of the unit, you will complete five exercises to improve your accuracy, write a timed essay to improve your fluency, and then explore topics for future writing.

Exercise 1 | Identifying facts and opinions

Write *F* if the statement is a fact. Write *O* if it is an opinion.

_____ 1. The Galápagos tortoise is the largest living tortoise.

_____ 2. Animals suffer when they are taken from the wild and put into zoos.

_____ 3. Scientists have evidence that birds are capable of complex thought.

_____ 4. Birds make great pets because they are friendly and intelligent.

_____ 5. The saguaro cactus is the most well-known of all desert plants.

_____ 6. Bats feed on the fruit of the saguaro cactus, which only blooms at night.

Exercise 2 | Recognizing counter-arguments and refutations

Read the statements below. Underline the counter-argument. Circle the writer's refutation.

1. Even though many people say they enjoy visiting bookstores, online shopping for books is becoming increasingly popular.

2. Not very many people actually ride in helicopters, so they might not think about them as important for our society; however, helicopters are necessary for many areas of city life, including news agencies, law enforcement, and emergency medicine.

3. The hydrogen-powered car is laughed at by many people because they think it is not possible to use water as fuel, but hydrogen-powered vehicles may help us solve serious environmental and political problems.

4. Day-care centers offer benefits to the children, their parents, and society even though there will always be people who disagree with them.

5. Many people consider a new type of rice as no big deal; however, the development of rice plants that are strong and resistant to disease can help prevent starvation in many countries.

6. Some people say that traveling to other countries is a waste of money, but international travel is worth the cost because it is fun and educational.

Understanding connectors

**Each of the sentences below has two clauses joined by a connector.
Write *O* for opposition if the clauses show opposing information or
S for support if they show supporting information, such as an example
or a similar idea.**

_____ 1. Kayaking can be a cold and wet sport; however, many people find it exciting and pleasurable.

_____ 2. A mall is a pleasant place to spend a Saturday afternoon; in fact, many people enjoy spending time at malls even if they are not shopping.

_____ 3. There are many inappropriate Web sites directed at teenage audiences; in contrast, Homestar Runner is an entertaining site that parents approve of.

_____ 4. It is true that some people become addicted to exercise; for example, I have a friend who feels anxious if she cannot work out at the gym every day.

_____ 5. A useful future invention would be one that replaces traditional keys and locks with something that recognizes fingerprints; in fact, most people would love this invention because they would not have to worry about losing or forgetting their keys.

_____ 6. Almost all parents want their children to get university degrees because they worry about their careers; however, there are many other ways that young people can become successful.

Identifying correct quantity expressions

Circle the correct quantity expression in the sentences below.

1. (Many / A lot) of equipment is needed for rock climbing.

2. There will always be (a few / a little) people that prefer to read a traditional printed book.

3. (Some / A little) instructions are so badly written that it is impossible to use them.

4. (A little / Many) allergies can be treated with over-the-counter drugs.

5. (Most / Many) job training involves actually doing a task.

6. Gyms usually have (a few / a little) space set aside for stretching.

Read the paragraph. Correct the mistakes with connectors. There are five mistakes.

Immigrants today have an easier life than immigrants of the past because communication and travel make it easier for us to stay connected to our countries. Homesickness and culture shock are big problems; in contrast, many people get very depressed if they cannot speak their language or communicate with their parents. In the past, people had letters and the telephone, but letters took a long time and the telephone was very expensive, so people had a long time to wait for communication. For example, e-mail allows today's immigrants to communicate as often as they want for free. E-mail has other advantages too; for example, I send photographs by e-mail, and my friend has a special video camera that she uses when she talks to her family. She can see them and they can see her. Another advantage for immigrants today is travel. People sometimes visited their country in the past, but it was a long and expensive trip; in fact, traveling overseas is easier nowadays because there are many flights and the tickets are not too expensive. I know many people who live in the United States, but they go back to their countries for special occasions; however, my friend went back two times last year for two different wedding celebrations. For an immigrant, going back home for a visit is the best cure for homesickness; in contrast, it sometimes helps them feel better about living in the new country. Although many people say that an immigrant's life is never easy, I am very glad that I live in these days and not fifty years ago.

 TIMED WRITING: 60 minutes

Write a three-paragraph opinion essay on the topic below. Before you begin to write, review the following time management strategy.

- Would you consider marrying someone from another culture?

Step 1　**BRAINSTORMING: 5 minutes**

Write down ideas and vocabulary for your essay on a separate piece of paper. You may want to use a chart similar to that on page 84.

Step 2　**OUTLINING: 5 minutes**

Write an outline for your essay.

Introduction

Hook: _____

_____

Background information: _____

_____

_____

Thesis statement: _____

_____

Body Paragraph

Topic sentence: _____

_____

_____

Example reasons: _____

_____

Counter-argument: _____

_____

Refutation: _____

_____

Conclusion

_____

_____

Step 3　**WRITING: 40 minutes**

Use your brainstorming notes and outline to write your first draft on a separate piece of paper.

Step 4　**EDITING: 10 minutes**

When you have finished your first draft, check it for mistakes using the checklist on page 104.

Editor's Checklist

Put a check (✓) as appropriate.

☐ 1. Does the essay have three paragraphs?

☐ 2. Does the introduction include a hook and a thesis?

☐ 3. Does the body paragraph have a topic sentence?

☐ 4. Does the body paragraph give reasons and explanations that support the topic sentence? Does it give a counter-argument and refutation?

☐ 5. Does the conclusion refer to the main idea of the essay?

☐ 6. Are quantity expressions used to avoid overgeneralizations?

☐ 7. Are connectors used to show the relationship (opposition or support) between ideas?

Topics for Future Writing

1. **Write a three-paragraph opinion essay on one of the following topics.**

   - A school policy that you agree with or disagree with
   - The best solution to overcoming traffic problems in your city
   - The biggest mistake that a college student can make
   - The ideal husband or wife

2. **Write a three-paragraph opinion essay on one of topics above, but from a friend's point of view. Interview a friend, classmate, or relative about his or her views on the topic. Take notes during the interview to use for your essay.**

3. **Use the Internet or other sources to research one of the following topics or a topic of your own choice. Then write a three-paragraph opinion essay.**

   - Hydrogen-powered vehicles
   - Testing in schools
   - Children and TV

Unit 5

Comparison and Contrast Essays

Unit Goals

Rhetorical focus:
- comparison and contrast organization

Language focus:
- comparison and contrast connectors
- using comparatives in comparison and contrast essays

PART 1

Stimulating Ideas

A comparison and contrast essay can be used to illustrate the similarities and differences between one idea or image and another. Often these comparisons help us to see the image or idea in a new way.

| Exercise 1 | **Thinking about the topic** |

A. Discuss pictures with a partner.

- Describe the scenes.
- How are they similar?
- How are they different?

B. In which of the two classes would you prefer to be a student? Why? Make notes and then discuss in small groups.

| Exercise 2 | **Reading about the topic** |

Sometimes living and working in another place can be quite a shock. In this article, award-winning economist Mohammad Yunus describes his experience as a PhD student in the United States.

Learning About Differences

Despite my success, I still wanted to study and teach. So when I was offered a Fulbright scholarship in 1965, I jumped at the chance to get a PhD in the United States. This was my third trip abroad. As a Boy Scout I had gone to Niagara Falls, Canada, in 1955 and to Japan and the Philippines in 1959. But this time I was on my own, and I was in for some surprises. At first the University of Colorado campus in Boulder was quite a shock. In Bangladesh, students never called professors by their first names. If one spoke to "sir," it was only after being invited by "sir" to speak, and then one spoke in **enormously** respectful terms. But in Boulder, teachers seemed to consider themselves friends of the students. I often saw faculty and students **sprawled out** on the lawn **barefoot**, sharing food, joking, and chatting. Such familiarity was totally unthinkable in Bangladesh. And as for the young female students in Colorado, well, I was so shy and embarrassed I did not know where to look. At Chittagong College, female students were the minority. Of a student body of eight hundred, no more than one hundred and fifty were women. Women were also **segregated**. They were usually confined to the Women's Common Room, which was off-limits to male students. Their participation in student politics and other activities was limited. When we staged plays, for example, women were not allowed to participate, so men wearing women's dress and makeup would take on female roles.

My female students at Chittagong University were extremely shy. When it was time for class, they would **huddle** in a group just outside the Teachers' Common Room and then follow me to class, **clutching** their books and looking down at their feet so as to avoid the stares of the boys. Inside the classroom they sat apart from the boys, and I learned not to ask them questions that could possibly embarrass them in front of their classmates. I never talked to them outside the classroom.

Yunus, M. *Banker to the Poor* (Adapted). New York: Public Affairs, 1999.

enormously: extremely
sprawled out: sitting or lying in a relaxed manner
barefoot: without shoes

segregated: separated
huddle: stand closely together
clutch: hold tightly

Understanding the text

Write *T* for true or *F* for false for each statement.

_____ 1. This was Yunus' first trip outside of Bangladesh.

_____ 2. The author was surprised by the University of Colorado students' behavior.

_____ 3. The author was eager to make friends with his female classmates in Colorado.

_____ 4. At Chittagong University, the author had more direct interaction with the female students than with the male students.

Responding to the text

Write your answers for each question in full sentences. Then discuss your answers with a partner.

1. How was communication between professors and students different at the University of Colorado than it was at Chittagong University? _____

_____

_____

_____

2. How did Yunus react to the young female students in Colorado? Why do you think this is so? _____

_____

_____

_____

3. According to the author, how was the experience of female students at Chittagong University different from that of male students? _____

_____

_____

_____

4. In this piece, Yunus is writing about an experience that he had in 1965. Has students' behavior changed over the last forty years or has it stayed the same? _____

_____

_____

_____

Write for ten to fifteen minutes on the topic below. Express yourself as well as you can. Don't worry about mistakes.

In this piece, Mohammad Yunus compares and contrasts his experiences at the University of Colorado at Boulder and at Chittagong University in Bangladesh. Think of two places you know well and compare them.

- Describe both places.
- How is the appearance of both places similar or different?
- How are the people similar or different?
- How are the customs and traditions of both places similar or different?

In Part 2 you will ...

- learn about comparison and contrast organization.
- brainstorm ideas and specific vocabulary to use in your writing.
- create an outline for your essay.

PART 2

Brainstorming and Outlining

✍ WRITING TASK

In this unit, you will write a three-paragraph comparison and contrast essay about two places you know. They could be places you have lived in or visited.

Exercise 1   Brainstorming ideas

A. Look at this Venn diagram and answer the questions below.

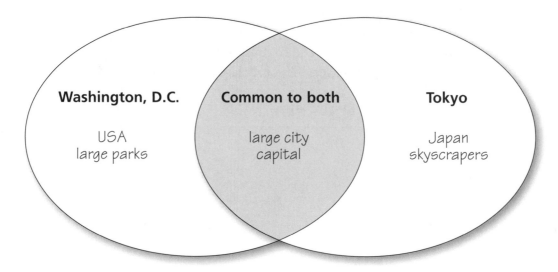

1. What two cities are compared in this diagram? _____
   _____

2. What are their contrasting characteristics? _____
   _____

3. What are their common characteristics? _____
   _____

B. Think of two places you want to write about. Then in your notebook, create your own Venn diagram. Use the diagram to list the characteristics that are unique to each place, as well as their common characteristics.

Brainstorming vocabulary

A. Use the chart below to categorize the adjectives according to the places they can describe.

stimulating	boring	lonely
tedious	competitive	filthy
energetic	peaceful	overwhelming

City	Rural Area	Beach	Bus Station

B. On a separate piece of paper, practice using these words in sentences. Use your dictionary for help.

Rhetorical Focus

Comparison and Contrast Organization

A comparison and contrast essay describes the qualities of a subject or idea by discussing the similarities and differences it shares with a different subject or idea.

A comparison and contrast essay can be organized in two different ways:

• By comparing and contrasting a number of issues point-by-point

• By focusing first on the similarities and then the differences.

Introduction
- Presents the subject that is to be compared or contrasted
- Ends with a thesis statement that focuses the comparison or contrast

Body Paragraphs for Point-by-Point Essays
- There are two body paragraphs, each with a clear topic sentence.
- Each body paragraph presents one main point to be compared or contrasted between the two subjects.
- Within each body paragraph, the topic sentence states the point of comparison or contrast between the subjects. The supporting sentences that follow provide two or three examples.
- The body paragraphs use sequence transitions, such as *first, second, furthermore,* etc., to connect the point-by-point analysis within the paragraph.

Body Paragraphs for Similarities and Differences Essays
- There are two body paragraphs, each with a clear topic sentence.
- One body paragraph is devoted to similarities between the two subjects, and one body paragraph is devoted to differences.

Conclusion
- This allows the writer to summarize the differences and similarities and state his or her feeling about the topic.

Exercise 3   **Reading a student essay**

Read the essay. What does Willowbrook Mall remind the writer of?

A Walk on Sunday Afternoon

I enjoy spending my Sunday afternoons outside the house. I cannot have the same experience in the United States that I had in Mexico when I was a child, but I have found a place that is similar to my home. Willowbrook Mall in Houston, Texas, is my favorite place in the U.S. to take a walk because it reminds me of Moreda Street in Morelia, Mexico. They are very different but also similar in some ways, especially on a Sunday afternoon.

For me, Willowbrook Mall has an atmosphere that is like Moreda Street's. In both places, people stroll and gather. In Morelia, families leave church and go for a walk along Moreda Street on Sunday afternoon. Often people stop at an outdoor café and have an ice cream or coffee and watch people walk by. Now that I live in Houston, Willowbrook Mall is the place where I go to see people on Sundays for their afternoon walk. I sit in a food court where I can drink a coffee with my friend, as I watch teenagers and families walking through the mall. When I see them, I remember how life was when I was a child.

Despite their similarities, Moreda Street and Willowbrook Mall are very different. Willowbrook Mall is more modern. On the one hand, Moreda Street has old colonial buildings and beautiful old trees that shade the street. It is also quiet. On the other hand, Willowbrook Mall is new and the lights are bright, and loud music plays in the stores. The people on Moreda Street also have more traditional ways. Men wear attractive, conservative suits and women wear light summer dresses. Fathers watch their teenage daughters closely and do not let their daughters hold hands with boys. In contrast, many teenagers go to Willowbrook Mall without their parents, and boyfriends and girlfriends walk with their arms around each other. When I see them, I realize that my daughter will have a different experience growing up in Houston than I did in Moreda. Then, I worry about her, and I miss Moreda Street, where life is more traditional.

It is interesting to see how people and places from different countries can be similar and different at the same time. Moreda Street and Willowbrook Mall are very different in appearance and culture, but they are also similar because they are both places where people like to go to relax on a Sunday afternoon.

Examining the student essay

A. Respond to the essay by answering the questions below in full sentences.

1. What does the writer like to do on Sunday afternoons? _____

   _____

2. Where did the writer go on Sunday afternoons in Morelia? _____

   _____

3. Where does the writer go in Houston? _____

   _____

4. What does the writer do in these places? _____

   _____

B. Now examine the organization of the essay. Answer the questions below. Then compare answers with a partner.

1. Is this a point-by-point essay or a similarities and differences essay?

   _____

2. Underline the thesis statement of the essay.

3. Write the topic sentence of the first body paragraph. In what way are the two places similar? _____

   _____

   _____

4. Write the topic sentence of the second body paragraph. In what way are the two places different? _____

   _____

   _____

5. Underline the sentence in the conclusion where the writer summarizes the main points.

Writing an outline

Review your brainstorming ideas and your freewriting exercise.
Then use the chart below to write an outline for your similarities and
differences essay. Remember to write your outline in note form. For
an outline of a point-by-point essay, see page 127.

Introduction

Two places to be compared:

1. _____ 2. _____

Hook: _____

_____

Thesis statement: _____

_____

_____

Body Paragraph 1

Topic sentence about similarities: _____

_____

Details: _____

_____

_____

Body Paragraph 2

Topic sentence about differences: _____

_____

Details: _____

_____

_____

Conclusion:

Summary sentence: _____

_____

_____

In Part 3 you will …

- learn about comparison and contrast connectors.
- write a first draft of your comparison and contrast essay.

PART 3

Developing Your Ideas

Reading a student essay

Read the essay. Which city does the author prefer?

My Two Homes

There are two places that have had a profound impact in my life. One of them is New York City, and the other is Quetzaltenango, Guatemala. When you compare them, they seem like dramatically different places, but they have some things in common, and I love them both.

There are many reasons why New York seems like my home away from home. Both cities are striking and distinctive. For example, each has its own nickname. Everyone knows New York is "the Big Apple." Quetzaltenango is known as "Xela" (pronounced shey-la), which is a lot easier to say! Second, both cities have a "Central Park" where people like to go and walk. Although Central Park in Xela is smaller, its tropical flowers and colonial architecture mean it is just as beautiful as New York's. Furthermore, when you walk around Xela, you find many tourists and people from other countries, just like in New York. For me, this means conversations in Xela are just as interesting as conversations in New York.

Despite their similarities, these cities are different. Life in Xela is more colorful and the pace of life is slower. For this reason, whenever I return to Xela, it is like an escape. When I arrive, the first thing I notice is the color. In New York, many people wear black to be stylish, but in Xela stylish clothing is the rainbow-colored clothing of the indigenous people. And because Xela is smaller, the beautiful green mountains outside the city are always visible. The second thing I notice is the pace of life. They say New York never sleeps, and it must be true, because I always see people walking and cars on the streets, even late at night. In the evening, my Guatemalan city definitely sleeps. Some younger people go out dancing and some families take a walk in the city's Central Park, but by ten o'clock the streets are pretty deserted. On the other hand, New Yorkers are often in such a hurry, they don't even stop to eat. For breakfast they buy food on the street, and eat it while they are walking or on the subway. At lunch they order food from work and eat at their desks. In Xela people eat their breakfast at home and most come home from work for a much more relaxed and longer lunch.

In conclusion, these are the two cities I love. For me, both are home, are unique, and are filled with interesting people. These places represent the best of both worlds. New York is more hurried and rushed when I need energy, and Xela gives me a slower pace when I need to relax. Together they keep me balanced.

Exercise 2   **Analyzing the student essay**

Respond to the essay by answering the questions below.

1. What two places does the author compare? _____

   _____

2. Write the thesis statement. _____

   _____

3. What do the two places have in common? _____

   _____

   _____

4. Re-read the second body paragraph. What details support the two points of contrast mentioned in the topic sentence of the paragraph?

   • Point of contrast 1 (color): _____

     _____

   • Point of contrast 2 (pace of life): _____

     _____

5. Look at the conclusion. In your own words, describe the writer's feelings about the two places. _____

   _____

   _____

Comparison and Contrast Connectors

In comparison and contrast essays, connectors help create coherence by indicating the relationship between ideas in sentences.

Connectors That Show Similarity

- Use connectors such as *like* (+ noun phrase) or *similarly* to show similarity.

  Like her sister, Angela was very tall.

  I grew up overseas in Shanghai. **Similarly**, my wife spent her childhood abroad in Laos.

Connectors That Show Contrast

- Use connectors like *unlike* (+ noun phrase), *in contrast*, or *on the one hand ... on the other hand* to show contrast.

  Unlike the fathers in Morelia, the fathers in Houston do not watch their teenagers as carefully.

  The pace of life in New York is very rapid. **In contrast**, life in Xela is slower.

  On the one hand, I enjoy the fast pace of New York. **On the other hand**, the pace of life in Xela relaxes me.

Exercise 3   **Using connectors to compare and contrast**

Rewrite the following sentences to show similarity or contrast. Choose the correct connector in parentheses to add more coherence.

1. Lemons are yellow. Limes are green. (unlike / similarly)

   _____

2. Many families can live in an apartment building. Only one or two families usually live in a house. (on the one hand ... on the other hand / like)

   _____

3. A frog can live in water or on land. A fish cannot. (like / unlike)

   _____

4. A parrot can fly. An ostrich cannot. (similarly / in contrast)

   _____

5. Rome is a city rich in history. Athens is too. (like / in contrast)

_____

6. Mozart composed his first opera at the age of 12. Mendelssohn composed his first masterpiece in his teens. (in contrast / similarly)

_____

Exercise 4   **Filling in connectors**

Complete the paragraph. Write *like, similarly, on the one hand ... on the other hand,* or *in contrast* in the blanks.

> The Eiffel Tower in Paris, France, and the Statue of Liberty in New York City may seem to be very different structures. However, they have many similarities. _____ the Eiffel Tower, the Statue of Liberty was designed by a French architect. _____, the Statue of Liberty and Eiffel Tower both represented great advancements in metalwork. The Eiffel Tower, however, is taller than the Statue of Liberty. The Eiffel Tower measures 986 feet. _____, the Statue of Liberty is only 305 feet from the water to the top of her torch. _____ you have the elegant black frame and sharp point of the Eiffel Tower, and _____ you have the long, flowing robes and lifelike torch of the Statue of Liberty. Both monuments are equally beautiful.

Exercise 5   **Writing a first draft**

Review your outline. Then write your first draft of a three-paragraph comparison and contrast essay on two places you know.

Peer editing a first draft

After you write your first draft, exchange it with a partner. Answer the questions on the checklist below. You may also write comments or questions on your partner's draft. Then read your partner's comments on your first draft, and revise it as necessary.

Editor's Checklist

Put a check (✓) as appropriate.

☐ 1. Does your thesis statement compare two subjects?

☐ 2. Does one body paragraph focus on comparison and one on contrast?

☐ 3. Does each body paragraph have a clear topic sentence?

☐ 4. Does each topic sentence state the point of comparison or contrast?

☐ 5. Does each body paragraph contain details to support the comparison or contrast?

☐ 6. Did you use connectors to add coherence?

In Part 4 you will …

- learn about using comparatives in comparison and contrast essays
- review comparatives in sentences.
- edit your first draft.

PART 4

Editing Your Writing

Now that you have written your first draft, it is time to edit. Editing involves making changes to your writing to improve it and correct mistakes.

Language Focus

Using Comparatives in Comparison and Contrast Essays

Comparison and contrast essays often use comparatives. Comparatives are used with adjectives, adverbs, and nouns to show differences between two subjects (people, objects, ideas, places, or actions).

Comparatives with Adjectives and Adverbs

- To form the comparative of one-syllable adjectives and adverbs, add *-er*. If the adjective or adverb ends in a single vowel and consonant, double the consonant.

- To form the comparative of most two-syllable adjectives and adverbs, add *more*; however, if the adjective ends in *-le*, use *-er*. If the adjective ends in a consonant plus *y*, change *y* to *i* and add *-er*.

Comparatives with Nouns

- To form the comparative of nouns, use *more*.

Comparative Forms of Adjectives, Adverbs, and Nouns

Adjectives		
ONE SYLLABLE	TWO SYLLABLES	THREE OR MORE SYLLABLES
tall - tall**er**	simple - simpl**er**	beautiful - **more** beautiful
cold - cold**er**	happy - happi**er**	expensive - **more** expensive
cute - cut**er**	famous - **more** famous	creative - **more** creative
big - bigg**er**	polite - polit**er** / **more** polite	intelligent - **more** intelligent

Adverb Regular Forms	
ONE SYLLABLE	TWO SYLLABLES
hard - hard**er**	quickly - **more** quickly
late - lat**er**	clearly - **more** clearly

Adverb Irregular Forms		
ADJECTIVE	ADVERB	COMPARATIVE
good	well	**better**
bad	badly	**worse**

Nouns			
COUNT NOUN	COMPARATIVE	NON-COUNT NOUN	COMPARATIVE
a book	**more** books	homework	**more** homework

Forming comparatives

Write the comparative form of the following adjectives and adverbs, using *-er* or *more*.

1. difficult _____

2. challenging _____

3. smart _____

4. tired _____

5. sleepy _____

6. energetically _____

Language Focus

Using Comparatives in Sentences

When we use a comparative in a sentence, we sometimes delete the second subject and verb. We also sometimes use the comparative without *than* when the context is clear. Look at the examples and charts below:

People in Xela are **less** stressed <u>than New Yorkers are</u>.
New Yorkers are always rushing around. People in Xela are **less** stressed.

Comparatives in Sentences

Comparatives with *than* and subjects			
	COMPARATIVE	*THAN*	SUBJECT (+ VERB OR AUXILIARY)
Lisa is	**taller**		her brother (is).
Tony works	**harder**	than	you (work). you (do).
We read	**more books**		they (do).

Comparatives with *than* and object pronouns			
	COMPARATIVE	*THAN*	OBJECT PRONOUN
Lisa is	**taller**		him.
Tony works	**harder**	than	you.
We read	**more books**		them.

Identifying comparatives

Underline the comparative in the sentences below.

1. Time passes <u>more slowly</u> in Xela <u>than</u> it does in New York.
2. The colonial buildings of Moreda Street are more beautiful than those in Willowbrook Mall.
3. The buildings in New York are taller than the buildings in Xela.
4. The parents on Moreda Street are more vigilant than the parents at Willowbrook Mall.
5. The clothing is more colorful in Xela than in New York.
6. The ice creams are bigger at Willowbrook Mall than in the cafés on Moreda Street.

Choosing the correct form of comparatives

Circle the correct form of the comparative in each sentence.

1. She was (very excited / more excited) than he was about the party.
2. Franz spoke (more enthusiastic / more enthusiastically) than Sabina about New York.
3. New York is much (cleaner / more clean) than it was a few years ago.
4. In Quetzaltenango the buildings are (older / more old).
5. My brothers are (taller / more tall) than I am, but my sisters are (shorter / more short).
6. Some people think that a beach vacation is (relaxier / more relaxing) than an adventure vacation.

Writing comparatives in sentences

Complete each sentence using a comparative. Use *-er, -ier, more,* or *less.*

1. A skyscraper is _____ than a sand dune.
2. Canada is _____ than Singapore.
3. A pizzeria is _____ than a four-star restaurant.
4. A baseball is _____ than a tennis ball.
5. A hospital is _____ than a medical clinic.
6. A library is _____ than a dance club.

Read the paragraph. Correct the mistakes with comparatives. There are eight mistakes.

> My old home is very different from where I live now. My old home was a house, but my new home is an apartment. My new apartment is more small than my old house, but the rooms are more large. Everyone in my family feels differently about this. My parents liked my old house because it was spaciouser, but I like the apartment because my room is more big. My brothers don't like the new apartment so much because they have to share a room. My older brother is more independent my younger brother, and so he wants his own room. My new apartment is also more close to the bus stop, so it is convenient than my old house, but it is also noisey.

Exercise 6   **Editing your first draft and rewriting**

Review your essay for mistakes. Use the checklist below. Then write a final draft.

Editor's Checklist

Put a check (✓) as appropriate.

☐ 1. Did you use comparatives in your essay?

☐ 2. Did you add -*er* to adjectives and adverbs with one syllable?

☐ 3. Did you add *more* to adjectives and adverbs with two or more syllables, and to nouns?

☐ 4. Did you use a different comparative pattern for irregular adverbs?

In Part 5 you will ...

• review the use of connectors and comparatives in comparison and contrast writing.

• write a timed comparison and contrast essay.

PART 5

Putting It All Together

In this part, you will complete four exercises to improve your accuracy, write a timed essay to improve your fluency, and then explore topics for future writing.

Exercise 1 — Using connectors to compare and contrast

Rewrite the following sentences using the correct connector in parentheses to add more coherence.

1. Vitamin C is water soluble. Vitamin D is not water soluble.
   (unlike / similarly)

   _____

2. I am short. My husband is tall. (in contrast / similarly)

   _____

3. CDs record only sound. DVDs contain sound and video. (on the one hand
   ... on the other hand / like)

   _____

4. A river is long and thin. A lake is wider, and usually deeper.
   (similarly / in contrast)

   _____

5. A dog can be a friendly pet. A cat is also friendly. (similarly / on the one
   hand ... on the other hand)

   _____

6. A friend can help you when you have problems. A brother or sister can, too.
   (like / unlike)

   _____

Exercise 2 — Forming comparatives

Write the comparative form of the following adjectives and adverbs, using *-er* or *more*.

1. difficult   _____
2. pretty   _____
3. exciting   _____
4. fast   _____
5. well   _____
6. spicy   _____

Identifying comparatives

Underline the comparative in the sentences below.

1. Computers today are more reliable than they were ten years ago.
2. Cars also run faster than they used to.
3. Americans today watch more TV than they did in the past.
4. Communication is more rapid than it once was.
5. International phone calls are also cheaper than they were just a few years ago.
6. This is making it easier than it once was for families to communicate across long distances.

Exercise 4   **Editing a paragraph**

Read the paragraph and edit as necessary. There are six mistakes.

> I like to go on public transportation whenever I can. Of course, private transportation is more comfortable public transportation in many ways. But I always feel more free when I travel on a bus or a train. I don't have to worry about parking and I can still go wherever I want. Also, taking buses and trains is interestinger. You meet more people and can spend more time enjoying the scenery. For me, this is much more relaxing driving my own car. I also find that I travel more light when I don't have my car, so life is more simpler than when I have lots and lots of suitcases and things to carry.

 TIMED WRITING: 60 minutes

Write a four-paragraph comparison and contrast essay on two people you know. Before you begin to write, review the following time management strategy.

Step 1   **BRAINSTORMING: 5 minutes**

Write down ideas and vocabulary for your brainstorm on a separate piece of paper. You may want to use a Venn diagram to do this.

Step 2   **OUTLINING: 5 minutes**

Write an outline for your essay in the form on page 127. Decide if you want to use a similarities and differences essay or a point-by-point essay. Use the appropriate outline for the body paragraphs.

Introduction

Hook: _____

_____

Background information: _____

_____

_____

Thesis statement: _____

_____

differences and similarities essay

Body Paragraph 1

Topic sentence about similarities: _____

_____

Details: _____

_____

_____

differences and similarities essay

Body Paragraph 2

Topic sentence about differences: _____

_____

Details: _____

_____

_____

point-by-point essay

Body Paragraph 1

Topic sentence with point of comparison: _____

_____

Details: _____

_____

_____

point-by-point essay

Body Paragraph 2

Topic sentence with point of comparison: _____

_____

Details: _____

_____

_____

Conclusion

Summary of points of comparison and contrast: _____

_____

_____

WRITING: 40 minutes

Use your brainstorming notes and outline to write your essay on a separate piece of paper.

EDITING: 10 minutes

When you have finished your essay, check it for mistakes using the checklist below.

Editor's Checklist

Put a check (✓) as appropriate.

☐ 1. Does the essay have four paragraphs?

☐ 2. Does the thesis statement that compare two subjects?

☐ 3. Does each body paragraph include details to support the topic sentence?

☐ 4. Does the essay include connectors to add coherence?

☐ 5. Does the essay use the correct form of comparatives?

☐ 6. Does the conclusion summarize the points of comparison and contrast?

Topics for Future Writing

1. Write a four-paragraph comparison and contrast essay on one of the following topics.

   - Two different pets
   - Two different celebrations
   - Two works of art
   - Two books that you have read

2. Write a four-paragraph essay on one of the topics above, but from a friend's point of view. Interview a friend, classmate, or relative about his or her views on the topic. Take notes during the interview to use for your essay.

3. Use the Internet or other sources to research one of the topics or a topic of your choice, then write a comparison and contrast essay based upon your research.

Unit 6

Cause and Effect Essays

Unit Goals

Rhetorical focus:
- cause and effect organization
- clustering information
- causal chains

Language focus:
- the future with *will*
- using *will* with *so that*
- expressing future possibilities with *if* clauses

PART 1

Stimulating Ideas

By analyzing causes, a writer explains why something happens. By analyzing effects, the writer explains the results or outcome of an event.

| Exercise 1 | **Thinking about the topic** |

A. Discuss the pictures above with a partner.

- Describe the scenes.
- Who is wealthier?
- How do you know?

B. Make notes about the ways in which people become wealthy. What lifestyle habits do you expect wealthy people to have? Then discuss in small groups.

| Exercise 2 | **Reading about the topic** |

The authors of this text report on their research into the lives and habits of millionaires and multi-millionaires in the United States.

The Millionaire Next Door

Who becomes wealthy? Usually the wealthy individual is a businessman who has lived in the same town for all of his adult life. This person owns a small factory, a chain of stores, or a service company. He has married once and remains married. He lives next door to people with much less money. He is a **compulsive** saver and investor. And he has made his money on his own. *Eighty percent of America's millionaires are first-generation rich.*

Affluent people typically follow a lifestyle **conducive** to **accumulating** money. In the course of our investigations, we discovered seven features among those who successfully build wealth.

1. They **live** well **below their means**.
2. They **allocate** their time, energy, and money efficiently, in ways conducive to building wealth.
3. They believe that financial independence is more important than displaying high social status.
4. Their parents did not allow them to become financially dependent.
5. Their adult children are economically **self-sufficient**.
6. They are good at finding opportunities to make money.
7. They chose the right job or career.

Stanley, T. *The Millionaire Next Door* (Adapted). New York: Pocket Books, 1996.

compulsive: doing something a lot and being unable to stop doing it
conducive: helpful in bringing about certain results
accumulate: to get and to save so that an amount of something grows
live below one's means: to spend less than one earns
allocate: to decide what resources (e.g., money) will be devoted to a particular purpose
self-sufficient: the ability to take care of one's self without depending on others.

Understanding the text

A. Write *T* for true or *F* for false for each statement.

_____ 1. A typical millionaire is easy to recognize by his beautiful house, his luxury car, and his expensive lifestyle.

_____ 2. Most millionaires are the first people in their family to become millionaires.

_____ 3. A typical millionaire is single.

_____ 4. A typical millionaire is more likely to enjoy saving and investing money than spending it.

Responding to the text

Write your answers for each question in full sentences. Then discuss your answers with a partner.

1. If you met a wealthy individual who matched the description in the passage, would he/she look rich? Why or why not? _____

_____

_____

_____

2. Describe the relationship this type of millionaire has with his family. Is it a positive relationship? Why or why not? _____

_____

_____

_____

3. What work habits does the typical millionaire have? Explain. _____

_____

_____

_____

4. What do you have in common with the typical millionaire? _____

_____

_____

_____

Write for ten to fifteen minutes on the topic below. Express yourself as well as you can. Don't worry about mistakes.

In the text, the writer describes people who are successful at accumulating wealth. On a separate piece of paper, write about your own experience managing your finances.

- Do you save money regularly?
- Do you live below your means?
- Does your family have an effective arrangement regarding money?
- Is financial success very important to you, or are you more interested in other types of success?

In Part 2 you will...

- learn about cause and effect organization.
- learn about clustering information.
- brainstorm ideas and specific vocabulary to use in your writing.
- create an outline for your essay.

Brainstorming and Outlining

✎ **WRITING TASK**

In this unit, you will write a four-paragraph cause and effect essay on the causes of some types of success. You may choose to discuss financial success or another type of success.

Exercise 1 **Brainstorming ideas**

A. The charts below show cause and effect relationships. In the blanks provided, write causes that lead to the particular event or situation.

Causes ⟶	Event or Situation
lots of friends	
	a successful party

Causes ⟶	Event or Situation
	a successful job interview

B. Think of a successful event or situation that you want to write about. Brainstorm the causes that lead to the event or situation and complete the chart below.

Causes ⟶	Event or Situation

Brainstorming vocabulary

  A. **Think about the type of success you want to write about. Add two more words to each set. Circle the words that you would like to use.**

  1. **Success:** fame, wealth, status,_____ ,_____

  2 **Actions:** succeed, accomplish, master,_____ ,_____

  3. **Qualities:** dedication, perseverance, hard work,_____ ,_____

  4. **Results:** bring about, result in, contribute to,_____ ,_____

  B. **On a separate piece of paper, practice using the words in sentences. Use your dictionary for help.**

Rhetorical Focus

Cause and Effect Organization

A cause and effect essay explains why something happens. Both causes and effects are examined in longer essays. Your short essay will focus only on causes that lead to an event or situation.

Introduction
- The hook engages the reader's interest by personalizing the topic or showing why it is important for the reader to know about it.
- The middle sentences describe the event or situation that is the result of the causes. This background information helps the reader understand the relationship between the causes and the effects.
- The thesis statement at the end of the introduction states two causes that lead up to the event or situation. It may also include a comment by the writer that explains why it is important to understand the causes of the event

Body Paragraphs
- There are two body paragraphs in the essay, which support the thesis statement by explaining the causes in detail.
- Each body paragraph begins with a topic sentence that states one cause for the event or situation.
- The sentences that follow support the idea in the topic sentence. These supporting sentences include details such as examples, description, reasons, and facts to help the reader understand the relationship between the cause and the event.

Conclusion
- The conclusion restates the thesis statement, often using different language.
- It summarizes the main causes and their relationship to the event.
- It may include a comment by the writer that explains why it is important to understand the causes of the event

Read the essay. According to the writer, what are the two main reasons that college students are poor?

Why Students Are Poor

It is easy to recognize a college student because he or she is carrying books and usually wearing old pants or jeans and a T-shirt. You will not see a college student driving a new car. Instead, you will see him at a bus stop or on a bicycle. And at mealtimes, a college student is more likely to be eating a slice of pizza than dining in a fine restaurant. Very few college students have extra money to spend on clothes, cars, or good food. There are two main reasons why being poor is an unavoidable part of the college experience.

The first reason college students are poor is that they cannot work full-time. An eighteen year-old is an adult with the needs and wants of an adult; however, if that young person is taking courses at a university or a community college, he or she must spend as much time as possible studying. Therefore, the student has to sacrifice the extra money that a job would provide in order to have the freedom to concentrate on classes.

A second reason college students have little money is that they have other expenses that working adults do not have. A college student must pay tuition fees every semester. A full-time student usually takes three or four classes each semester, and the fees for these classes can cost thousands of dollars per year. Also, students need to buy several expensive textbooks each semester. A single textbook can cost as much as a hundred dollars. Other necessary expenses include computers, paper, pens, notebooks, and other items needed for school projects.

Many students cannot afford to attend college full-time, so they have a job and go to school part-time, but they are still poor because of the cost of attending college. Fortunately, the causes of student poverty are temporary. Most students do not mind because they have the hope that a college degree will get them a good job and they will have good prospects in the future.

Analyzing the student essay

A. Respond to the essay by answering the questions below in full sentences.

1. What details would you add to or change in the writer's description of a college student? _____

_____

2. Why do college students sacrifice the extra money that a job would provide?

_____

_____

3. What are the additional expenses that college students have? _____

_____

4. Explain whether you think the writer admires college students or not, and why. _____

_____

B. Examine the organization of the essay by answering the questions below. Then compare your answers with a partner.

1. How does the writer catch the reader's attention?

   a. with an example that the reader is familiar with

   b. with a surprising fact or statistic

   c. with a short narrative to set the context

2. Put a check next to the background information that appears in the introduction.

   _____ a. what a college student wears

   _____ b. where a college student lives

   _____ c. what a college student eats

   _____ d. what kind of transportation a college student uses

3. How many causes will be discussed, according to the thesis statement? _____

4. Does the thesis statement directly state what the causes are? _____

5. Underline the topic sentences of each body paragraph.

6. Do the topic sentences support the thesis statement? _____

7. Is each topic sentence supported with reasons and explanations?
   _____

8. How does the writer comment on the information?
   a. suggests a change or solution   b. gives an opinion

Rhetorical Focus

Clustering Information

The product of a brainstorming activity is a set of ideas, but the ideas are not necessarily organized in the order in which they will appear in the final essay. Clustering is the process of grouping ideas that are similar so that the writer can develop the information into a thesis statement, topic sentences, and supporting details.

Exercise 5   **Clustering ideas**

A. **Look at the first chart below. The writer has brainstormed ideas for a cause and effect essay. He has then eliminated irrelevant or problematic ideas. In the second chart, cluster ideas using the two categories provided.**

Causes	Event or Situation
~~luck~~ ~~a good coach~~ a strong body no injuries fast decisions cooperation with other players ~~have lots of equipment~~ being fast / agile ~~a good diet~~ stress management	becoming a successful professional athlete

Mental Clarity	Physical Strength
• _____	• _____
• _____	• _____
• _____	• _____

B. **Look at your brainstorming ideas from page 136. On a separate page, cluster your ideas into logical categories.**

Developing ideas into an outline

Look at the outline elements below. Answer the questions that follow.

Thesis Statement

The factors that determine if an individual can have a successful career in professional sports include physical ability and mental clarity.

Body Paragraph 1	**Body Paragraph 2**
In order to become a professional athlete, a person must be athletically gifted. • a strong body • speed • no injuries	Another factor that contributes to a successful career in sports is a strong mind. • manage stress • make fast strategic decisions • cooperate with team members

1. Read the thesis statement. According to the writer, what two causes lead to success in professional sports? _____

_____

2. How has the writer organized the two body paragraphs? _____

_____

3. What is the topic in body paragraph 1? _____

_____

4. What is the topic in body paragraph 2? _____

_____

5. What is the topic in body paragraph 1? _____

_____

6. How do the details support the topic sentences?
   a. The provide descriptions.   b. They give facts and statistics.

Writing an outline

Review your brainstorming ideas and your freewriting exercise. Then use the chart below to write an outline for your essay. Remember to write your outline in note form.

Introduction

Hook: _____

_____

_____

Background information: _____

_____

_____

Thesis statement: _____

_____

_____

Body Paragraph 1

Topic sentence: _____

_____

_____

Supporting detail: _____

_____

_____

Supporting detail: _____

_____

_____

Supporting detail: _____

_____

_____

Body Paragraph 2

Topic sentence: _____

_____

_____

Supporting detail: _____

_____

_____

Supporting detail: _____

_____

_____

Supporting detail: _____

_____

_____

Conclusion

Restatement of thesis: _____

_____

_____

Summary and/or comment: _____

_____

_____

_____

In Part 3 you will ...

- learn about causal chains.
- write a first draft of your cause and effect essay.

Reading a student essay

Read the essay. Name two things that are necessary to become a professional athlete.

What It Takes to Be a Professional Athlete

At this moment, somewhere in the world a young boy is dreaming about becoming a famous soccer player. He has posters of famous soccer stars in his room, and every day he goes out to practice with his friends. He even cuts his hair in the same style as his favorite player. Thousands of young people feel the same as this boy. However, only a few children actually become professional athletes. The factors that determine if an individual can have a successful career in professional sports include physical ability and mental clarity.

In order to become a professional athlete, a person must be athletically gifted. This means the athlete must be stronger than others. A soccer star should be able to run faster and farther that most other athletes. A basketball player has to be able to fake, block, and shoot while other powerful players are trying to stop him. Athletes need the support of their families. Finally, in order to make a career out of sports, the player must be able to prevent injuries. Many young athletes have to quit because they have sports injuries. It is very difficult to play a sport year after year and not get seriously hurt. So a powerful, agile, and resilient body is essential.

The other factor that contributes to a successful career in sports is a strong mind. An athlete must be able to manage stress and to focus on the game. A tennis player might feel a lot of stress, which could interfere with her ability to concentrate. She might hit the ball out of bounds. A crowd of people yelling at a baseball pitcher might make him throw balls instead of strikes. To succeed, an athlete must be able to play under this kind of pressure. Athletes need the right kind of equipment to perform at their peak. In addition, an athlete must be able to make quick strategic decisions. Making the right decision to pass or shoot, for example, is extremely important, especially in team sports. Finally, an athlete must be able to cooperate with his team members. So even though he might want to keep the ball and make all the shots, he must focus on passing the ball to the player who has the best chance of scoring. He cannot think only about himself if he wants his team to win.

In conclusion, the two contributing factors to a successful career in athletics are physical ability and a strong mind and character. Therefore, children who want to become famous athletes should take care of their bodies and practice every day. In addition, they should develop their minds so that they can be cooperative players in whatever game they eventually play.

Exercise 2 **Examining the student essay**

Examine the organization of the essay by answering the questions below. Then compare your answers with a partner.

1. Underline the hook. Which of the following strategies is used?

   a. personalization   b. surprising statement   c. famous quote

2. What background information do you learn in the first paragraph?

   _____

   _____

3. Circle and label the thesis statement. Does it focus on causes or effects?

4. According to the thesis statement, how many main causes (or effects) will be discussed? _____

5. Does the thesis statement directly mention the causes (or effects)? _____

6. Underline and label the topic sentence of each body paragraph.

7. Draw a line through the sentence in each body paragraph that does not support the topic sentence of that paragraph.

8. Does the author restate the thesis statement in the conclusion? _____

9. What type of comment does the writer make in the conclusion?

   a. a warning   b. advice   c. a prediction

Rhetorical Focus

Causal Chains

Sometimes the causes of an event happen in a sequence in which one event leads to another in a chain. Depending on the event or situation, the writer must explain how the causes in a chain are related to each other. Look at the causal chain below. Then read the short passage that follows to see how this chain was developed into a paragraph.

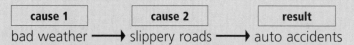

cause 1	cause 2	result

bad weather ⟶ slippery roads ⟶ auto accidents

Auto accidents occur more frequently when the weather is bad. Rain, snow, and especially ice can make the roads slippery. Drivers can easily lose control of a car on slippery roads. A car can slide on the pavement and hit another car or go into a ditch. Therefore, bad weather can lead to more accidents on the road.

Notice that in the passage above, bad weather does not cause accidents directly: bad weather leads to slippery roads, which then create conditions for auto accidents to happen.

Exercise 4 Recognizing related causes in a causal chain

A. Number the causes below so that they form a logical causal chain.

1. _____ a. The industry creates good jobs.

   _____ b. Many people move to the city to take the jobs.

   _____ c. An industry is developed in a city.

   Result: The price of housing goes up.

2. _____ a. Caffeine acts as a stimulant.

   _____ b. A person drinks a lot of soda.

   _____ c. The caffeine in the soda goes into the person's bloodstream.

   Result: The person cannot sleep.

3. _____ a. The job applicant does well in the job interview.

   _____ b. The job applicant researches the requirements of the position, and prepares carefully.

   _____ c. The job applicant arrives 10 minutes early to the interview.

   Result: The job applicant gets the job.

4. _____ a. Food is left out overnight.

    _____ b. The person eats the food.

    _____ c. Bacteria begins to grow in the food.

Result: The person gets sick.

5. _____ a. The supply of oil decreases.

    _____ b. Oil production comes to a halt.

    _____ c. A powerful storm damages an oil refinery.

Result: The price of gasoline goes up.

B. Choose one of the causal chains from A, then develop the chain into a short paragraph.

_____

_____

_____

_____

_____

_____

_____

_____

Exercise 5   **Writing a first draft**

Review your outline. Then write the first draft of a four-paragraph essay on the causes of some type of success. You can choose financial success or another type of success.

After you write your first draft, exchange it with a partner. Answer the questions on the checklist. You may also write comments or questions on your partner's draft. Then read your partner's comments on your first draft, and revise it as necessary.

Editor's Checklist

Put a check (✓) as appropriate. Write answers in complete sentences in the lines provided.

☐ 1. Does the essay have four paragraphs?

☐ 2. Does the introduction include a hook to get the reader's attention?

☐ 3. Do the connecting sentences describe the event or situation that is the result of the causes? Write the event or situation below:

_____

☐ 4. Is there a thesis statement that focuses the essay? Does it mention two causes that lead to the situation?

☐ 5. Does each body paragraph have a topic sentence that states one cause mentioned in the thesis statement?

☐ 6. Do supporting sentences in each body paragraph explain the cause in the topic sentence of that paragraph?

☐ 7. Does the conclusion summarize the causes and comment on them?

In Part 4 you will...

- learn about the use of future with *will*.
- learn about using *will* with *so that*.
- learn about future possibility with *if* clauses.
- edit your first draft.

PART 4

Editing Your Writing

Now that you have written a first draft, it is time to edit. Editing involves making changes to your writing to improve it and correct mistakes.

Language Focus

The Future with *Will*

In a cause and effect essay, you will need to discuss future effects of a cause or set of causes. The modal *will* is often used to talk about the future.

- Use *will* to make predictions. You can also use adverbs like *probably* or *certainly* with *will* to express a degree of certainly.

  He **will win** the race.
  He **will** <u>probably</u> **be** wealthy one day.

- *Will* is followed by the base form of the verb.

- Use the same form of *will* with any subject.

Future with *will*			
SUBJECT	**WILL (+ NOT)**	**BASE FORM OF THE VERB**	
I		be	rich.
You			
She	will	have	success.
We	will not		
You		save	money.
They			

Exercise 1 **Making predictions with *will***

Finish the following sentences to make predictions. Use *will* or *will not*.

1. A talented actor <u>will probably become famous.</u>

_____

2. A hardworking student _____

_____

3. A dedicated employee _____

_____

4. An overworked and exhausted doctor _____

_____

5. An employee who has a lot of personal problems _____

_____

6. A person who wants to be a millionaire _____

_____

Language Focus

Using *Will* with *So That*

- The future with *will* can also be used with the logical connector *so that*. In this type of sentence, the main clause uses the simple present and states the cause. It is followed by *so that* and a second main clause with *will*.

main clause (present)		time clause (future)
Students work hard in school	**so that**	they **will be** successful.

Exercise 2   **Using *will* with *so that***

Rewrite the sentences below using *so that* and *will*.

1. Some drivers drink a lot of caffeinated drinks in order to stay awake.

   Some drivers drink a lot of coffee so that they will stay awake.

   _____

2. Students sacrifice many things in order to save money for school.

   _____

   _____

3. Many stores advertise sales in order to attract customers.

   _____

   _____

4. Many people pay bills online in order to save money and time.

   _____

   _____

5. Some people carpool to work in order to save money.

_____

_____

6. Many people work very hard in order to be successful.

_____

_____

Language Focus

Expressing Future Possibility With *If* Clauses

Sentences with an *if* clause show a cause-and-effect relationship. The *if* clause introduces a possible situation (the cause). The main clause talks about the possible result (the effect) of the situation.

- Use the present tense in the *if* clause and *will* in the main clause.

cause		effect

If X happens, Y **will happen,** too.

- The cause and effect clauses can come in either order. When the *if* clause comes first, it is followed by a comma.

if clause		main clause

If Pedro plays,   we **will win** the game.

main clause		*if* clause

We **will win** the game   **if** Pedro plays.

⚠ Do not use *will* in the *if* clause.

If the price of oil will increase, people will drive less. (INCORRECT)
If the price of oil increases, people will drive less.

Exercise 3   **Forming *if* clauses**

Combine the ideas below so that they form one sentence with an *if* clause.

1. (money managers / be discipline / achieve financial goals)
   <u>If money managers are disciplined, they will achieve financial goals.</u>

2. (applicant / interview well / receive job offers)

   _____

   _____

3. (you / exercise regularly / be healthy in old age)

   _____

   _____

4. (restaurant / serve delicious food / be successful)

_____

_____

5. (I / work hard / be promoted)

_____

_____

6. (parents / be good at solving problems / be successful at raising children.)

_____

_____

7. (she / invests money wisely / become wealthy)

_____

_____

8. (students / study hard / graduate college)

_____

_____

Exercise 4   **Editing a paragraph**

Read the paragraph and edit as necessary. There are two mistakes in punctuation, and four mistakes in verb form.

Camping is an inexpensive and fun choice for a family vacation. However, camping trips can end in disaster. The first problem is usually a lack of preparation. If the campers do not make a list they will probably forget something important. And they are sorry if they do not have the right equipment. Another problem is bad weather. The campers will have to check into a motel, if it rains. Camping in the rain is never fun. Finally, insects will to ruin a vacation easily. Mosquitoes will make an evening meal out of any unprotected camper and then he will scratching for days afterward. In conclusion, wise campers will know how to prepare so that they will not being surprised by these unfortunate causes of disaster.

Exercise 5 Editing your first draft and rewriting

Review your essay for mistakes. Use the checklist below. Then write a final draft.

Editor's Checklist

Put a check (✓) as appropriate.

☐ 1. Did you use correct verb tenses?

☐ 2. Did you include predictions? Did you follow the rules for using *will* correctly?

☐ 3. Did you use *so that* to show cause and effect relationships?

☐ 4. Did you use *if* clauses to show cause and effect?

☐ 5. Did you check the punctuation?

In Part 5 you will...

• review the elements of writing a cause and effect essay.
• write a timed cause and effect essay.

PART 5

Putting It All Together

In this part of the unit, you will complete five exercises to improve your accuracy, write a timed essay to improve your fluency, and explore topics for future writing.

Exercise 1   **Recognizing related causes in a causal chain**

Number the causes so that they form a logical casual chain.

1. _____ a. A worker loses his job.

   _____ b. The worker borrows money from the bank to pay bills.

   _____ c. The worker is unable to pay his bills.

   Result: The worker goes into debt.

2. _____ a. Water is rationed.

   _____ b. Communities have to use water reserves.

   _____ c. An area receives less than average rainfall.

   Result: Water supplies are depleted. A drought is declared.

3. _____ a. Children don't do their homework.

   _____ b. Children fail their exams.

   _____ c. Children watch too much TV.

   Result: Children have to take summer school.

4. _____ a. Tourism becomes very popular in the village.

   _____ b. Road are built to a remote village in India.

   _____ c. Many new hotels are built and forests are cut down.

   Result: Animals living around the village lose their natural habitat.

Exercise 2   **Making predictions with *will***

Finish the following sentences to make predictions. Use *will* or *will not*.

1. A person who wants to lose weight _____

   _____

2. A terrible teacher _____

   _____

3. A careful driver _____

   _____

4. A vegetarian _____

_____

5. A dishonest salesperson _____

_____

6. A successful politician _____

_____

Using *will* with *so that*

Rewrite the sentences below using *will* and *so that*.

1. Many people exercise in order to be healthy.

_____

_____

2. Many nurses wear special shoes in order to be comfortable.

_____

_____

3. Many immigrants work hard in order to be successful in their new country.

_____

_____

4. Many homeowners have alarm systems in order to feel safe.

_____

_____

5. Many older people have pets in order to not feel lonely.

_____

_____

6. Many schools offer financial aid in order to attract new students.

_____

_____

Forming *if* clauses

Combine the ideas below so that they form one sentence with an *if* clause.

1. (a person / work as an international pilot / travel to other countries)

_____

_____

2. (you / learn another language / feel a sense of accomplishment)

_____

_____

3. (you / have good computer skills / be qualified for many good jobs)

_____

_____

4. (a person / practice yoga / feel more energetic)

_____

_____

5. (you / plan your vacation carefully / have fewer problems during your trip)

_____

_____

6. (a person / respect others / have a lot of friends)

_____

_____

Exercise 5   **Editing a paragraph**

Read the following essay. There are six mistakes.

Children who participate in sports will be more successful in their jobs. First of all, team sports require kids to play together with their team. In this way, they will to learn cooperation skills. For example, while playing soccer a child might realize that a teammate has a better chance of scoring a goal. If he will pass the ball to his teammate, he will not control it any more. However, his teammate will probably score a goal. By learning to cooperate on the playing field the child will one day be more efficient employee. In addition, children who play team sports will learning how to be good sports. If the team will lose a game, the child remembers that it is only a game. Instead of getting upset, he will to try to do better next time. And when he works for a company, he will not to get upset if he loses an important client or sale.

TIMED WRITING: 60 minutes

Write a four-paragraph cause and effect essay on the topic below. Before you begin to write, review the following time management strategy.

- What causes people to get a pet, such as a cat or dog?

Step 1 **BRAINSTORMING: 5 minutes**

Write down ideas and vocabulary for your brainstorm here or on a separate piece of paper. You may want to cluster your ideas.

Step 2 **OUTLINING: 5 minutes**

Write an outline for your essay.

Introduction

Hook: _____

_____

_____

Background information: _____

_____

_____

Thesis statement: _____

_____

_____

Body Paragraph 1

Topic sentence: _____

_____

_____

Supporting detail: _____

_____

_____

Supporting detail: _____

_____

_____

Supporting detail: _____

_____

_____

Body Paragraph 2

Topic sentence: _____

_____

_____

Supporting detail: _____

_____

_____

Supporting detail: _____

_____

_____

Supporting detail: _____

_____

_____

Conclusion

Summary: _____

_____

_____

Comment: _____

_____

_____

Step 3 **WRITING: 40 minutes**

Use your brainstorming notes and outline to write your essay on a separate piece of paper.

Step 4 **EDITING: 10 minutes**

When you have finished your first draft, check it for errors, using the checklist on page 157.

Editor's Checklist

Put a check (✓) as appropriate. Write answers in complete sentences in the lines provided.

☐ 1. Does the essay have four paragraphs?

☐ 2. Does the introduction include a hook and background information that explains the effect of the causes, or the event or situation that has effects?

☐ 3 Is there a thesis statement that focuses the essay? Does it mention two causes that lead to the situation/effects that are the outcome of a situation?

☐ 4. Does each body paragraph have a topic sentence that states one cause or effect mentioned in the thesis statement?

☐ 5. Do supporting sentences in each body paragraph explain the cause or effect in the topic sentence of that paragraph?

☐ 6. Does the conclusion summarize the causes and comment on them?

☐ 7. Did you include predictions? Did you follow the rules for using *will* correctly?

☐ 8. Did you use *if* clauses to show cause and/or effect?
   Comments:

   _____

   _____

   _____

Topics for Future Writing

1. **Write a four-paragraph cause and effect essay on one of the following topics.**

   • What causes insomnia (not being able to sleep at night)?
   • What causes students to cheat on tests?
   • What are the main causes of problems between friends?

2. **Interview a friend or classmate about his or her views on one of the topics above. Using your notes, write a four paragraph cause and effect essay from his or her point of view.**

3. **Use the Internet or other sources to research one of the topics or a topic of your own choice, and write a cause and effect essay based upon your research.**

Appendices

Appendix I: **The Writing Process**

1. Brainstorming

Before you begin to write, gather information about the topic. Then, brainstorm ideas and vocabulary related to the topic. Read your assignment carefully so that your finished product will meet your instructor's expectations.

▶ **Strategies:** Read about the topic and discuss it with your classmates. Look at pictures or diagrams, to help you come up with ideas.

2. Creating an outline

Decide which ideas you will use in your essay. Cluster ideas into logical parts. This may be in the form of a chart, a web, or a list of main ideas. Write an outline or plan for your paper.

▶ **Strategies:** Look at models that are similar to the writing that you want to do. Learn ways to organize and sequence your ideas. Create a visual plan for your paper.

3. Writing a First Draft

Expand your outline into a draft by rewriting your notes into full sentences. At this stage, don't worry about mistakes. When you have finished, ask a classmate to read your work and give you feedback.

▶ **Strategies:** Evaluate your outline as you write. Take out ideas that do not support your argument; add clarification or examples. Check your work to make sure your writing is clear and accomplishes the goals of the assignment.

4. Editing

Now apply your knowledge of grammar and mechanics, and correct any mistakes that you notice. Review the feedback you received from your classmates.

▶ **Strategies:** Separate yourself from the ideas so that you can focus on clarity at the sentence level. If possible, put your paper aside for a few hours before you edit. Read your essay sentence by sentence. (Some writers read a paper backwards so as not to be distracted by content.)

5. Writing a Final Draft and Submitting Your Work

Rewrite your draft so that it looks neat and has all the features of a finished college paper. Some writers type their papers; others write by hand.

▶ **Strategies:** Make sure your paper has the correct format. Make sure your name and the date are on the paper, and that there is a title.

Appendix II: **Punctuation**

Commas

A comma (,) is used to separate information from other parts of the sentence.

1. A comma is used to separate items in a series. Use *and* before the last item if listing three or more items.
   - We made rice, chicken, salad, and cake.

2. A comma is used to separate an introductory word or phrase.
   - At the end of the day, my husband and I sit on the sofa and talk about our day.

3. A comma is used after a dependent clause when the dependent clause precedes (or introduces) an independent clause.
   - When the power went off, we could not listen to the radio.

4. A comma is used to separate two main clauses when there is a conjunction such as *and, but,* or *so* shows a relationship between them.
   - The temperature was below freezing, but we were warm.

5. A comma is used to separate an appositive from the rest of the sentence. An appositive appearing after any noun in a sentence is set off with commas.
   - We used to visit North Beach, a Bohemian neighborhood in San Francisco.
   - The speaker, an Ecuadorian economist, supported his points with facts and statistics.

Periods

Periods (.) are used to mark the end of a sentence.

- She speaks four languages.

Colons

Colons (:) are used to introduce a list of items. They can be particularly helpful when writing thesis statements because they allow the writer to introduce the major ideas.

Colons must be preceded by an independent clause. They can be followed by a group of words, phrases or, in some cases, clauses.

- In order to build a tree house, you will need the following items: nails, a hammer, boards, and a tape measure.

Semicolons

Semicolons (;) are used at the end of a sentence. They follow the same rules as periods; however, they are only appropriate if the relationship between the two sentences is close.

1. Semicolons are used between two separate sentences.
    *   They help each other; she does the bookkeeping while he takes care of customers.

2. Semicolons are used when two sentences are joined by a connector such as *however*, or *therefore*.
    *   The Earth's oceans still hold many secrets; however, new technology is helping scientists to understand them better.

Apostrophes

Apostrophes (') are used to show possession.

1. When a noun is singular, add an apostrophe and *s* to show possession. In the first example, the writer has one cousin.
    *   We went to my cousin's house.

2. When a noun is plural, put the apostrophe after the plural *s*. In the next example, the writer has more than one cousin.
    *   We went to my cousins' house.

3. When a noun ends in s, you may add the apostrophe + *s* after the final s or just the apostrophe.
    *   My boss' car was ridiculously expensive.
    *   My boss's car was ridiculously expensive.

Apostrophes are also used in contractions. (Note, however, that contractions are not appropriate in most academic writing.)

*   Scott doesn't have any hair.

Quotation Marks

Quotation marks ("...") are used to show that you are repeating or quoting someone else's words.

Put quotation marks around only the exact words you take from someone else's speech or writing. Use a comma to separate the quote from the rest of the sentence.

*   I heard him say, "Don't worry about the report, Mr. Noor. I will take care of it."

Appendix III: **Connectors**

Giving Examples	
CONNECTORS	EXAMPLES
for example *for instance*	• My best friend is so loyal; **for example,** she flies to Miami every year to visit me. • The Polish language is grammatically quite different from English. **For instance,** it does not have articles.

Showing Contrast / Differences	
CONNECTORS	EXAMPLES
but *yet* *while* *even though* *although* *however* *in contrast* *unlike* *on the one hand* *… on the other* *hand*	• I wanted to talk to her, **but** I was afraid of her brothers. • He never finished college, **yet** he became a millionaire at the age of twenty-five. • **While** many large cats are almost extinct, the number of African lions is on the rise across the continent. • **Even though** he did not attend school, he taught himself to read and write. • **Although** the Guggenheim museum has a modern appearance, it fits into the old architecture of Bilbao very well. • We expected good weather; **however,** it rained very hard all day. • I have seven siblings; **in contrast,** my husband is an only child.

Giving Reasons	
CONNECTORS	EXAMPLES
so *because*	• I was distracted by the stars, **so** I didn't see the big puddle. • I used to eat a lot of fish **because** we lived next to the ocean.

Showing Results	
CONNECTORS	EXAMPLES
therefore *consequently*	• This new technology presents many risks to the patient; **therefore,** many doctors prefer more traditional treatments. • Our house was on a small hill; **consequently,** we were safe during the flood.

Adding Information

CONNECTORS	EXAMPLES
and *in addition* *moreover*	• The hotel was built on a cliff, **and** it had marvelous views of the ocean. • Deforestation poses a threat to many native species. **In addition,** the construction of a large factory in the area is causing great environmental damage. • We were lost in the forest; **moreover,** it was getting dark.

Showing Similarities

CONNECTORS	EXAMPLES
similarly *likewise* *like*	• Hollywood makes a variety of movies that are distributed around the world; **similarly,** Mumbai makes movies for international export. • My brother entered the Navy after college; **likewise,** his wife joined the Navy at the age of twenty-two.

Showing Time Relationships

CONNECTORS	EXAMPLES
while *when* *before* *after* *after that* *meanwhile* *then* *finally*	• I listen to the radio **while** I chat online. • We were getting ready to go to my grandfather's house **when** my father's friends showed up. • **Before** the game began, the umpire flipped a coin. • **After** I count the money and put it in the safe, I can close the store and go home. • I count the money and put it in the safe. **After that,** I can close the store and go home. • Bring the water to a boil. **Meanwhile** prepare the rest of the ingredients. • Add the salts to the solution, and **then** stir carefully until they have fully dissolved. **Finally,** heat the mixture to 50 degrees Celsius.

Drawing Conclusions

CONNECTORS	EXAMPLES
in conclusion *in summary*	• **In conclusion,** there are surprising similarities in men and women's attitudes towards marriage. • Unemployment is very high. Interest rates are going up, and the rate of inflation is on the increase. **In summary,** the president's economic reforms do not seem to be working.

Appendix IV: **Glossary**

Adapted from the **Grammar Sense** *Glossary of Grammar Terms*

action verb A verb that describes a thing that someone or something does. An action verb does not describe a state or condition.

> Sam **rang** the bell.
> It **rains** a lot here.

active sentence In active sentences, the agent (the noun that is performing the action) is in subject position and the receiver (the noun that receives or is a result of the action) is in object position. In the following sentence, the subject **Alex** performed the action, and the object **letter** received the action.

> Alex mailed the letter.

adjective A word that describes or modifies the meaning of a noun.

> the **orange** car   a **strange** noise

adverb A word that describes or modifies the meaning of a verb, another adverb, an adjective, or a sentence. Many adverbs answer such questions as *How? When? Where?* or *How often?* They often end in **-ly.**

> She ran **quickly**.   She ran **very** quickly.
> a **really** hot day   **Maybe** she'll leave.

adverbial phrase A phrase that functions as an adverb.

> Amy spoke **very softly**.

affirmative statement A sentence that does not have a negative verb.

> Linda went to the movies.

agreement The subject and verb of a clause must agree in number. If the subject is singular, the verb form is also singular. If the subject is plural, the verb form is also plural.

> **He comes** home early.   **They come** home early.

article The words **a, an,** and **the** in English. Articles are used to introduce and identify nouns.

> **a** potato   **an** onion   **the** supermarket

auxiliary verb A verb that is used before main verbs (or other auxiliary verbs) in a sentence. Auxiliary verbs are usually used in questions and negative sentences. **Do, have,** and **be** can act as auxiliary verbs. Modals (**may, can, will,** and so on) are also auxiliary verbs.

> **Do** you have the time?   The car **was** speeding.
> I **have** never been to Italy.   I **may** be late.

base form The form of a verb without any verb endings; the infinitive form without *to.*

> sleep   be   stop

clause A group of words that has a subject and a verb. *See also* **dependent clause** and **main clause.**

> If I leave, ... when he speaks.
> The rain stopped.   . . . that I saw.

common noun A noun that refers to any of a class of people, animals, places, things, or ideas. Common nouns are not capitalized.

> man   cat   city   pencil   grammar

comparative A form of an adjective, adverb, or noun that is used to express differences between two items or situations.

> This book is **heavier than** that one.
> He runs **more quickly than** his brother.
> A CD costs **more money than** a cassette.

complex sentence A sentence that has a main clause and one or more dependent clauses.

> When the bell rang, we were finishing dinner.

compound sentence A sentence that has two main clauses separated by a comma and a conjunction, or by a semi-colon.

> She is very talented; she can sing and dance.

conditional sentence A sentence that expresses a real or unreal situation in the *if* clause, and the (real or unreal) expected result in the main clause.

> If I have time, I will travel to Africa.
> If I had time, I would travel to Africa.

countable noun A common noun that can be counted. It usually has both a singular and a plural form.

> orange — oranges   woman — women

definite article The word **the** in English. It is used to identify nouns based on assumptions about what information the speaker and listener share about the noun. The definite article is also used for making general statements about a whole class or group of nouns.

> Please give me **the** key.
> **The** scorpion is dangerous.

dependent clause A clause that cannot stand alone as a sentence because it depends on the main clause to complete the meaning of the sentence. Also called *subordinate clause.*

> I'm going home **after he calls**.

determiner A word such as **a, an, the, this, that, these, those, my, some, a few,** and **three** that is used before a noun to limit its meaning in some way.

> **those** videos

future A time that is to come. The future is expressed in English with **will, be going to,** the simple present, or the present continuous. These different forms of the future often have different meanings and uses.

> I **will** help you later.
> David **is going to** call later.
> The train **leaves** at 6:05 this evening.
> I**'m driving** to Toronto tomorrow.

gerund An **-ing** form of a verb that is used in place of a noun or pronoun to name an activity or a state.

> **Skiing** is fun.   He doesn't like **being sick**.

***if* clause** A dependent clause that begins with **if** and expresses a real or unreal situation.

> **If I have the time,** I'll paint the kitchen.
> **If I had the time,** I'd paint the kitchen.

indefinite article The words **a** and **an** in English. Indefinite articles introduce a noun as a member of a class of nouns or make generalizations about a whole class or group of nouns.

> **An** ocean is **a** large body of water.

independent clause *See* **main clause.**

indirect object A noun or pronoun used after some verbs that refers to the person who receives the direct object of a sentence.

> John wrote a letter to **Mary**.
> Please buy some milk for **us**.

infinitive A verb form that includes **to** + the base form of a verb. An infinitive is used in place of a noun or pronoun to name an activity or situation expressed by a verb.

> Do you like **to swim**?

intransitive verb A verb that cannot be followed by an object.

> We finally **arrived**.

main clause A clause that can be used by itself as a sentence. Also called *independent clause*.

> I'm going home.

main verb A verb that can be used alone in a sentence. A main verb can also occur with an auxiliary verb.

> I **ate** lunch at 11:30.
> Kate can't **eat** lunch today.

modal The auxiliary verbs **can, could, may, might, must, should, will,** and **would**. They modify the meaning of a main verb by expressing ability, authority, formality, politeness, or various degrees of certainty. Also called *modal auxiliary*.

> You **should** take something for your headache.
> Applicants **must** have a high school diploma.

negative statement A sentence with a negative verb.

> I **didn't see** that movie.

noun A word that typically refers to a person, animal, place, thing, or idea.

> Tom   rabbit   store   computer   mathematics

noun clause A dependent clause that can occur in the same place as a noun, pronoun, or noun phrase in a sentence. Noun clauses begin with **wh-** words, **if, whether,** or **that.**

> I don't know **where he is**.
> I wonder **if he's coming**.
> I don't know **whether it's true**.
> I think **that it's a lie**.

noun phrase A phrase formed by a noun and its modifiers. A noun phrase can substitute for a noun in a sentence.

> She drank **milk**.
> She drank **chocolate milk**.
> She drank **the milk**.

object A noun, pronoun, or noun phrase that follows a transitive verb or a preposition.

> He likes **pizza**.   Go with **her**.
> She likes **him**.   Steve threw **the ball**.

passive sentence Passive sentences emphasize the receiver of an action by changing the usual order of the subject and object in a sentence. In the sentence below, the subject **(The letter)** does not perform the action; it receives the action or is the result of an action. The passive is formed with a form of **be** + the past participle of a transitive verb.

> The letter was mailed yesterday.

past continuous A verb form that expresses an action or situation in progress at a specific time in the past. The past continuous is formed with **was** or **were** + verb + **-ing**. Also called *past progressive*.

> A: What **were** you **doing** last night at eight o'clock?
> B: I **was studying**.

past participle A past verb form that may differ from the simple past form of some irregular verbs. It is used to form the present perfect, for example.

> I have never **seen** that movie.

phrasal verb A two- or three-word verb such as **turn down** or **run out of**. The meaning of a phrasal verb is usually different from the meanings of its individual words.

> She **turned down** the job offer.
> Don't **run out of** gas on the freeway.

phrase A group of words that can form a grammatical unit. A phrase can take the form of a noun phrase, verb phrase, adjective phrase, adverbial phrase, or prepositional phrase. This means it can act as a noun, verb, adjective, adverb, or preposition.

> The **tall man** left.   She spoke **too fast**.
> Lee **hit the ball**.   They ran **down the stairs**.

preposition A word such as **at, in, on,** or **to,** that links nouns, pronouns, and gerunds to other words.

prepositional phrase A phrase that consists of a preposition followed by a noun or noun phrase.

> on Sunday   under the table

present continuous A verb form that indicates that an activity is in progress, temporary, or changing. It is formed with **be** + verb + **-ing.** Also called *present progressive*.

> I**'m watering** the garden.
> Ruth **is working** for her uncle.

present perfect A verb form that expresses a connection between the past and the present. It indicates indefinite past time, recent past time, or continuing past time. The present perfect is formed with **have** + the past participle of the main verb.

> I**'ve seen** that movie.
> The manager **has** just **resigned**.
> We**'ve been** here for three hours.

pronoun A word that can replace a noun or noun phrase. **I, you, he, she, it, mine,** and **yours** are some examples of pronouns.

quantity expression A word or words that occur before a noun to express a quantity or amount of that noun.

> **a lot of** rain   **few** books   **four** trucks

simple past A verb form that expresses actions and situations that were completed at a definite time in the past.

> Carol **ate** lunch.   She **was** hungry.

simple present A verb form that expresses general statements, especially about habitual or repeated activities and permanent situations.

> Every morning I **catch** the 8:00 bus.
> The earth **is** round.

stative verb A type of verb that is not usually used in the continuous form because it expresses a condition or state that is not changing. **Know, love, see,** and **smell** are some examples.

subject A noun, pronoun, or noun phrase that precedes the verb phrase in a sentence. The subject is closely related to the verb as the doer or experiencer of the action or state, or closely related to the noun that is being described in a sentence with *be*.

> **Erica** kicked the ball.
> **The park** is huge.

subordinate clause *See* **dependent clause.**

superlative A form of an adjective, adverb, or noun that is used to rank an item or situation first or last in a group of three or more.

> This perfume has **the strongest** scent.
> He speaks **the fastest** of all.
> That machine makes **the most noise** of the three.

tense The form of a verb that shows past, present, and future time.

> He **lives** in New York now.
> He **lived** in Washington two years ago.
> He**'ll live** in Toronto next year.

time clause A dependent clause that begins with a word such as **while, when, before,** or **after.** It expresses the relationship in time between two different events in the same sentence.

> **Before Sandy left,** she fixed the copy machine.

time expression A phrase that functions as an adverb of time.

> She graduated **three years ago**.
> I'll see them **the day after tomorrow**.

transitive verb A verb that is followed by an object.

> I **read** the book.

uncountable (noncount) noun A common noun that cannot be counted. A noncount noun has no plural form and cannot occur with **a, an,** or a number.

> information   mathematics   weather

verb A word that refers to an action or a state.

> Gina **closed** the window.
> Tim **loves** classical music.

verb phrase A phrase that has a main verb and any objects, adverbs, or dependent clauses that complete the meaning of the verb in the sentence.

> Who **called you**?
> He **walked slowly.**

Appendix V: **Correlation to *Grammar Sense 2***

EFFECTIVE ACADEMIC WRITING 2 THE SHORT ESSAY	GRAMMAR SENSE 2
Unit 2 Use and formation of adjectives Order of adjectives	**Chapter 16** Adjectives
Unit 3 Past continuous Verb forms in past time clauses	**Chapter 5** The Past Continuous and Past Time Clauses
Unit 4 Quantity expressions	**Chapter 14** Nouns and Quantity Expressions
Unit 5 Using comparatives in compare and contrast sentences Comparatives in sentences	**Chapter 18** Comparatives and Superlatives
Unit 6 Future with *will* *Will* in *if clauses* *Will* + *so that*	**Chapter 7** Future Time: *Be Going To, Will,* and the Present Continuous **Chapter 8** Future Time Clauses and *If* Clauses